MANTRA FOR THE MODERN MAN
and other
Heart-to-Heart Talks

J. P. Vaswani

Other Books By Dada J. P. Vaswani

In English:

10 Commandments of A Successful Marriage
108 Pearls of Practical Wisdom
108 Simple Prayers of A Simple Man
108 Thoughts on Success
114 Thoughts on Love
A Little Book of Life
A Simple and Easy Way to God
A Treasure of Quotes
Around The Camp Fire
Begin The Day With God
Bhagavad Gita in a Nutshell
Burn Anger Before Anger Burns You
Dada Answers
Daily Inspiration
Daily Inspiration (Booklet)
Destination Happiness
Dewdrops of Love
Does God Have Favourites?
Formula For Prosperity
Gateways to Heaven
God In Quest of Man
Good Parenting
How to Overcome Depression and other Heart-to-Heart Talks
I Am A Sindhi
In 2012 All Will Be Well
Joy Peace Pills
Kill Fear Before Fear Kills You
Ladder of Abhyasa
Lessons Life Has Taught Me
Life After Death
Management: Moment by Moment
Mantras For Peace Of Mind
Many Paths: One Goal
Nearer, My God, To Thee!
New Education Can Make The World New
Peace or Perish
Positive Power of Thanksgiving
Sadhu Vaswani: His Life And Teachings
Saints For You and Me
Saints With A Difference
Secrets of Health And Happiness
Shake Hands With Life
Short Sketches of Saints Known & Unknown
Sketches of Saints Known & Unknown
Spirituality In Daily Life
Stop Complaining: Start Thanking!
Swallow Irritation Before Irritation Swallows You
Teachers Are Sculptors
Ten Companions of God
The Goal of Life and How to Attain it
The Little Book of Freedom From Stress
The Little Book of Prayer
The Little Book of Service
The Little Book of Success
The Little Book of Wisdom
The Little Book of Yoga
The Magic of Forgiveness
The Miracle of Forgiving
The New Age Diet: Vegetarianism For You And Me
The Perfect Relationship: Guru and Disciple
The Seven Commandments of The Bhagavad Gita
The Terror Within
The Way of Abhyasa (How To Meditate)
Thus Have I Been Taught
Tips For Teenagers
What to do When Difficulties Strike
What You Would Like To Know About Hinduism
What You Would Like To Know About Karma
Why Be Sad?
Why Do Good People Suffer?
Women: Where Would The World Be Without You?
You Are Not Alone God Is With You!
You Can Change Your Life

Story Books:

101 Stories For You And Me
100 Stories You Will Never Forget
25 Stories For Children and Also For Teens
Break The Habit
It's All A Matter of Attitude
Snacks For The Soul
More Snacks For The Soul
The Lord Provides
The Heart of a Mother
The King of Kings
The One Thing Needful
The Patience of Purna
The Power of Good Deeds
The Power of Thought
Trust Me All in All or Not at All
Whom Do You Love The Most
You Can Make A Difference

In Hindi:

Aalwar Santon Ki Mahaan Gaathaayen
Aapke Karm, Aapka Bhaagya Banaate Hai
Aatmik Jalpaan
Aatmik Poshaan
Bhakton Ki Uljhanon Kaa Saral Upaai
Bhale Logon Ke Saath Buraa Kyon?
Brindaavan Kaa Baalak
Dainik Prernaa
Dar Se Mukti Paayen
Ishwar Tujhe Pranaam
Jiski Jholi Mein Hain Pyaar
Krodh Ko Jalaayen Swayam Ko Nahin
Laghu Kathaayein
Mrutyu Hai Dwar... Phir Kyaa?
Nava Pushp (Bhajans In Hindi and Sindhi)

Praarthna Ki Shakti
Pyar Kaa Masihaa
Sadhu Vaswani: Unkaa Jeevan Aur Shikshaayen
Safal Vivah Ke Dus Rahasya
Santon Ki Leela
Shammaa Karoge Shukhi Rahoge
Srimad Bhagvad Gita: Gagar Ma Sagar

In Sindhi:
Burn Anger Before Anger Burns You
Jaade Pireen Kaare Pandh
Munhinjee Dil Ta Lagee Laahootiyun Saan
Why Do Good People Suffer
Vatan Je Varnan De

In Marathi:
Krodhalaa Shaanth Karaa, Krodhane Ghala Ghalnya Purvee (Burn Anger Before Anger Burns You)
Jiski Jholi Mein Hai Pyaar
Life After Death
Pilgrim of Love
Sind and the Sindhis
Sufi Sant (Sufi Saints of East and West)
What You Would Like To Know About Karma

In Kannada:
101 Stories For You And Me
Burn Anger Before Anger Burns You
Life After Death
Tips for Teenagers
Why do Good People Suffer

In Telugu:
Burn Anger Before Anger Burns You
Life after Death
What You Would Like To Know About Karma

In Arabic:
Daily Appointment With God
Daily Inspiration

In Chinese:
Daily Appointment With God

In Dutch:
Begin The Day With God

In Bahasa:
A Little Book of Success
A Little Book of Wisdom
Burn Anger Before Anger Burns You
Life After Death

In Spanish:
Aprenda A Controlar Su Ira (Burn Anger Before Anger Burns You)
Bocaditos Para el Alma (Snacks For The Soul)
Dios (Daily Meeting With God)
El Bein Quentu Hagas, Regresa (The Good You Do Returns)
Encontro Diario Con Dios (Daily Appontment With God)
Inicia Tu Dia Con Dios (Begin The Day With God)
L'Inspiration Quotidienne (Daily Inspiration)
Mas Bocaditos Para el Alma (More Snacks For The Soul)
Mata Al Miedo Antes De Que El Miedo Te Mate (Kill Fear Before Fear Kills you)
Queme La Ira Antes Que La Ira Lo Queme A Usted(Burn Anger Before Anger Burns You)
Sita Diario Ku Dios (I Luv U, God!)
Todo Es Cuestion De Actitud! (Its All A Matter of Attitude)
Vida Despues De La Muerte (Life After Death)

In Gujarati:
It's All A Matter of Attitude

In Oriya:
Burn Anger Before Anger Burns You
More Snacks For The Soul
Pilgrim of Love
Snacks For The Soul
Why Do Good People Suffer

In Russian:
What Would You Like To Know About Karma

In Tamil:
10 Commandments of a Successful Marriage
Burn Anger Before Anger Burns You
Daily Appointment with God
Its All a Matter of Attitude
Kill Fear Before Fear Kills You
More Snacks For The Soul
Secrets of Health And Happiness
Snacks For The Soul
Why Do Good People Suffer

In Latvian:
The Magic of Forgiveness

Other Publications:

Recipe Books:
90 Vegetarian Sindhi Recipes
Delicious Vegetarian Recipes
Simply Vegetarian

Books on Dada J. P. Vaswani:
A Pilgrim of Love
Dada J.P. Vaswani: His Life and Teachings
Dada J.P. Vaswani's Historic Visit to Sind
Dost Thou Keep Memory?
How To Embrace Pain
Living Legend
Moments with the Master

STERLING PAPERBACKS
An imprint of
Sterling Publishers (P) Ltd.
A-59, Okhla Industrial Area, Phase-II,
New Delhi-110020.
Tel: 26387070, 26386209; Fax: 91-11-26383788
E-mail: mail@sterlingpublishers.com
www.sterlingpublishers.com

Mantra For The Modern Man and Other Heart-to-Heart Talks
© 2013, J. P. Vaswani
ISBN 978 81 207 8431 4

All rights are reserved.
No part of this publication may be reproduced, stored in a retrieval system or transmitted, in any form or by any means, mechanical, photocopying, recording or otherwise, without prior written permission of the original publisher.

DADA VASWANI BOOKS
Visit us online to purchase books on self improvement, spiritual advancement, meditation and philosophy. Plus audio cassettes, CDs, DVDs, monthly journals and books in Hindi.
www.dadavaswanisbooks.org

Printed in India
Printed and Published by Sterling Publishers Pvt. Ltd.,
New Delhi-110 020.

Contents

The Story of Pundalik 7

Three Great Gifts Of Life 19

The Monarch Who Became A Mystic 29

The Blessings of Guru-Bhakti 39

Awakening the Kundalini 49

The Four Gatekeepers to the Kingdom of God 59

A Thief Called Temptation 69

The Transformation of Francis 78

Happiness, Where is Thy Abode? 88

What Am I? 98

Wherever There is Beauty, There is GOD 107

Mantra For The Modern Man 117

No One Belongs to Us 127

The World is a Bridge 136

The Gift God Needs 145

The Guru leads us out of the darkness of *moha* and *maya* into the light of detachment and peace.

The Story of Pundalik

The *Taittriya Upanishad* tells us: *Matru devo bhava! Pitru devo bhava!* Revere your father and mother even as you revere God!

In a traditional *Gurukul* type of school in Kerala, the authorities had recently organised a simple ceremony to uphold this teaching. It was a symbolic *padha puja* of all the parents, by their own children. One of the parents who attended the ceremony was so touched by this symbolic act of devotion, that he was moved to tears. He became aware that he had failed to respect and revere his own mother, thus causing a severe strain on their relationship. When he left the school, he drove to the old age home where his mother resided. Wordlessly, he fell at her feet and begged her forgiveness.

"I do not believe in rituals, mother," he said to her. "But the ceremony at my son's school has opened my eyes to my own deficiencies as a son. Please forgive me for all the hurt I have caused you by my indifference and apathy. I know that the mere act of washing your feet will not take me far. But I offer my tears at the altar of your heart. Please forgive your erring son."

The mother had indeed been hurt and disappointed by her son's behaviour in the past. But this spontaneous gesture touched her heart, and she assured her son that all was forgiven. He begged her to leave the Retirement Community and return home with him; but this, she declined, as she was in a spiritually conducive environment in the *ashram* of a saint, with opportunities for *satsang* and a meditative life, which suited her time of life.

Dear friends, Retirement Communities and Senior Citizens' Homes were unheard of, fifty years ago. But now they are springing up in every nook and corner of the country. It does not speak well of us, as a nation and a society!

It is not enough to chant *Matru devo bhava! Pitru devo bhava!* It is not enough to perform rituals that are merely external. But it is important to bear witness to the great scriptural injunctions in deeds of daily life.

Tum mata pita, hum balak tere! We sing with deep emotion. I shudder to think what will become of our relationship with God if some of us begin to treat Him with the scant respect and care we give to our parents!

Have you ever considered what your existence would have been like, if you had been born as a dog, a cat, a fox or even a mosquito? According to the Hindu theory of *karma*, we could be born as any of these creatures, depending on our *karma*. But we have been born as human beings, with the unique body-mind complex with its six senses. And the people who are responsible for bestowing this physical form upon us are none other than our parents. Biologically, genetically and emotionally, we are linked to them in this birth, in one of the strongest bonds of this human life. They gave us birth, and the scriptures equate them to God on this earth. *Matru devo bhava! Pitru devo bhava!*

Our parents are the first visible representatives of God on earth. As we evolve towards higher consciousness, the Guru assumes the role of God in our lives. And in the next phase of spiritual growth, we begin to look upon God as our Father and Mother.

We owe this great gift of the human birth to our parents. The English idiom expresses this vital truth in the words: our children are our flesh and blood. We are nurtured in the womb of the mother, before we take birth. This is our physical birth. There is another birth we take – our spiritual birth. Yes; each of us is born twice. Once, out of the darkness of the mother's womb; and the other, out of the darkness of the world. The second birth, I refer to as our spiritual birth – because it leads us out of the darkness of ignorance to the world of light, knowledge and truth. It is the grace of God and the Guru that leads us out of darkness into the realm of light. Therefore, it is but apt that we look upon the Guru as our true mother and father. In his turn, the Guru teaches us that we are all children of the One Father, God. One relationship does not contradict the other, nor cancel out the other! As we grow in the love of God and the Guru, we also grow in the consciousness that we have duties towards our parents which we must not neglect on any account!

Do we not read of Adi Shankara, that even after becoming a great *acharya*, he broke the traditions of *sannyasa* to keep his promise to his mother to return to her during the last few hours of her earth pilgrimage, and perform her *antim samskaras* as a son?

Friends, it is not the rules and rituals that are important, but the spirit in which they are obeyed or performed. As a *sannyasi*, Shankara was not permitted to perform any *samskaras*. Yet he broke the tradition to teach us the great truth that a son's filial obligations are as sacred as his spiritual attainments.

Gurudev Sadhu Vaswani too, faced a predicament very similar to that of Sri Shankara. As a young man, he was drawn to the life of the Spirit, and was keen to renounce worldly life and become an ascetic, a *fakir*. But his mother simply would not hear of it! She reminded Sadhu Vaswani that he had obligations to fulfill as her son, and he implicitly obeyed her wish. It was only after she passed away that he gave up his successful academic career as a Principal, and took to the life of the Spirit.

We owe a deep debt of devotion and gratitude to our parents. Sri Rama himself demonstrated this in his incarnation. The great *avatara purushas* have borne witness to the fact that our duty towards our parents must not be neglected on any account.

At his physical birth, man is born into a world of material pleasures. As a child, he is entranced by all kinds of toys, and when he grows up, he discovers the many pleasures of the senses, of sight, sound and taste. He becomes the slave of his taste buds, and thinks nothing of killing dumb, defenceless creatures to satisfy his appetite. He lusts after the world's great sources of temptation – wealth, women, wine, power, position and fame. When the lust and craving grow out of proportion, he sins, and he sins in more than one way. It is a familiar story that we see enacted all around us. The great Gujarati saint Narsi Mehta called it *moha maya*, attachment to an illusion. In one of his songs he says:

> He does not succumb to worldly attachments;
> He has devoted himself to staunch detachment from worldly pleasures;

> He is addicted to the elixir of the Name of God;
> For him all the sacred places of pilgrimage are in the mind;
> He has no greed and is not deceitful;
> He has renounced lust and anger.
> The poet Narsi would like to see such a person
> By whose virtue, his entire family attains salvation.

How may we be liberated from the sins of the senses? How may we escape the deadly snare of the temptations of the flesh? How may we come to realise the truth that the pleasures of the senses are just illusory shadows?

The answer is simple: it is only an evolved soul, a realised soul who can awaken us to the reality of the self and the purpose for which we have been given this human birth. At the feet of such an evolved spiritual guide, we are born again. To such a Guru, we sing in Gurudev Sadhu Vaswani's immortal words:

> Thou art my father, my mother Thou art,
> I know no closer relationship or bond.

Let me explain: the Guru does not expect you to sever your bonds with your parents. Not at all! Parents have their rightful and highly respected place in our lives. It is our duty to revere them; to obey them, and to serve them to the best of our ability. We should never ever forsake our duties to our parents. For they have brought us into this world. They have cared for us when we were helpless and utterly dependent on them for everything we needed. They have given us unconditional love and support in our growing years. They have nurtured and helped us to grow into young adults and mature individuals. They are our biological parents, our flesh and blood. But deep within us, lies the hidden consciousness that we are children of God, the Father as well as the Mother of all the Universe. It is the

Guru who awakens us to this memory and gives us our second birth – the spiritual birth.

There was a saint who would exhort his disciples to remember that heaven is at the feet of your mother and father. It is the son's duty to serve his parents. But remember too, he added, that your true birth is when you step into the spiritual world.

Let me tell you the story of a holy man who came into the realisation of both these great truths at one and the same time. He took spiritual birth and realised that heaven was at the feet of his parents at the same moment of divine consciousness!

This is the beautiful story of Pundalik, the beloved saint of Pandharpur in Maharashtra. We have several versions of his life-story as sung by various contemporary saints like Janabai and Bahinabai. Pundalik, in his early years, was a man of the world. His parents got him married to a beautiful woman. He was so madly in love with her, that he began to dance to her tune and neglected his ageing parents. He spent most of his time in the pleasurable company of his spouse, turning a blind eye to the old couple's needs.

Dear ones, we would do well to bear in mind that one new relationship cannot cancel out another! When our younger brothers or sisters are born, our parents don't love us any less! But young people today make this mistake: they make marriage an excuse for neglecting their parents. They are so absorbed by their marital life, they begin to ignore the origin and source of their own life on earth! So it was with Pundalik. He was like a slave to his wife, and his parents were completely forgotten!

May I say something to you: in their old age, our parents do not want money or lavish gifts from us. All they need is a little bit of our time, so that we may sit beside them and reaffirm our love and affection for them. They need this reaffirmation to know that they are loved and wanted, and not forgotten by their children. This is exactly what Pundalik failed to do!

In despair and sorrow, the old couple decided to leave on a pilgrimage to Kashi. As you know, from the days of yore, pious Indians believe that Kashi is the threshold to liberation from the wretched miseries of worldly life and the endless cycle of birth and death. Pundalik's parents too decided that they would seek escape from their sorrows at Kashi. But they were not destined to undertake this last pilgrimage in peace. At the eleventh hour, Pundalik's wife decided that she too would join them, so that they may serve her and cater to her needs on the long journey. Pundalik promptly bought two fine horses; he and his wife rode the horses, while his old parents walked beside them. When they halted for the night, Pundalik and his wife would fall asleep, while the old couple had to groom and feed the horses and get them ready for the morrow's journey. They rued their fate; they rued the day that they had decided to leave on the pilgrimage to Kashi, to escape from the neglect of their son and daughter-in-law. They were now trapped in serving her and fulfilling her every whim and fancy.

It was a long way to Kashi! One night, they arrived at the *ashram* of a holy man, who offered them food and shelter for a couple of days, before they proceeded on their pilgrimage. Pundalik thanked the saint and enquired if he had had the *darshan* of Lord Vishwanath at Kashi. The saint replied that he had not visited Kashi. Feeling very superior, Pundalik whispered to his wife, "He calls himself a *sadhu*, and has an *ashram*! And he has not taken the trouble to visit Kashi!"

The *ashram* was an oasis of peace and tranquility. Pundalik spent a pleasurable night in the company of his wife, while his old parents slept in the open courtyard of the *ashram*. Early in the morning, as he awoke, Pundalik saw a strange vision; three young women entered the *ashram*. Their clothes were dirty and soiled and they appeared disheveled and unkempt. They swept and cleaned the *ashram*, and washed the saint's clothes. Then they gathered flowers and took them into the *puja* room. When they emerged from the *puja* room they were utterly transformed! Their robes shone in splendour, they looked utterly radiant and divinely beautiful. They left the *ashram* as quietly as they had entered.

Speechless with wonder, Pundalik decided to stay on at the *ashram* for one more day. He could barely sleep the following night, keeping awake lest he should miss the arrival of the mysterious women. Sure enough, they arrived early the next morning. Pundalik rushed to meet them as they emerged from the *puja* room, in all their radiance and splendour.

"Who are you?" he demanded eagerly. "How is it that you enter the portals of this *ashram* looking like menials, and leave as if you were royalty? And what is it about this place that brings about such a miraculous transformation in you?"

The eldest woman spoke to him in reply. "I am Ganga," she said to him, "and these are my sisters, Yamuna and Saraswati. Everyday thousands of men and women wash away their sins in our waters and we are defiled and polluted by the stain of their sins. We come here to clean the *ashram* of this holy saint, and his grace and blessings purify us and restore us to our pristine condition as sacred rivers. It is his magnanimity that has permitted us to offer our *seva* to him, for our own benefit."

Pundalik was stunned. "You call this man a saint with such miraculous powers, but he has not visited Kashi even once!"

"He does not need to go to Kashi," Ganga replied. "The sacred waters wash his feet right here, for he was a devoted and obedient son to his parents, and spent all his youthful life in their loving service. By fulfilling his filial obligations, he has attained tremendous spiritual stature, and deserves to be in the heaven-world. God has kept him here, so that he may guide other wandering souls back to the path. We come to him for purification and grace."

The women turned to leave, but Ganga had a few parting words for him. "As for you, Pundalik, you are the greatest sinner among them all! Not even a visit to Kashi or a dip in our holy waters can wash you of the sin of neglecting your parents!"

Pundalik was stunned! He saw his life in a flash before him and realised how grievous was the injury that he had inflicted on his parents. He fell at the feet of the holy man, and begged forgiveness. "Who am I to forgive you?" laughed the saint. "Fall at the feet of your parents and beg for their forgiveness. In serving them is your salvation!"

In an instant, Pundalik was free from the snare of *moha maya*! The pilgrimage to Kashi was forgotten. He realised that he had a long way to go, before he thought of salvation. He returned to Pandharpur and turned over a new leaf. "I am no longer your slave," he said to his wife. "My first duty is to my parents, whom I have neglected sadly all these years! My parents are old and they need me. I am blessed with a new life and the opportunity to serve them."

From then on, Pundalik devoted himself utterly and completely to the loving service of his parents. As they grew old and frail, his loving care and attention to their needs increased manifold. Such a devotion to duty pleases the Lord above all else. Sri Krishna saw the selfless service and filial piety of this evolved soul, and came with His divine consort, Rukmini, to visit Pundalik at Pandharpur.

Arriving at the cottage door, he called out, "Pundalik! Pundalik! Are you there? We have come to visit you, My wife and I."

"Who is it?" called Pundalik, busy washing his father's feet.

"It is I, Krishna. Rukmini is with Me."

"Dear Lord, You will have to wait till my duty is done. Why don't You stand on this brick for a while, so that Your feet don't get muddy," said Pundalik throwing a couple of bricks at the door. In all obedience, Sri Krishna and Rukmini stood patiently on the bricks, till Pundalik completed washing his father's feet.

When he finally emerged from his house, he was elated to see the Lord waiting patiently to give him *darshan*. He fell at Sri Krishna's feet, and begged forgiveness. But Sri Krishna assured him that it was his devotion to his parents that had brought the divine couple to his doorstep. Such was the Lord's love for His devoted *bhakta* that He ordained that a shrine should be built for him at the very spot where He and Rukmini stood on their bricks. Thus did the famous

Pandharpur temple come into being, and Sri Krishna is worshipped here as Vitthoba – the Lord who stands on a brick.

Pundalik was awakened to the truth by the grace of his Guru, and blessed by the grace of Sri Krishna. His fame spread far and wide. He was illumined by the Divine Light. He had borne witness in deeds of daily life, to the great scriptural saying: *Matru devo bhava! Pitru devo bhava!*

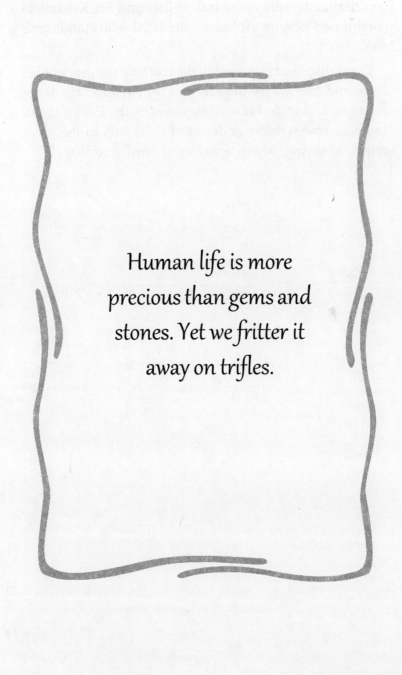

Human life is more precious than gems and stones. Yet we fritter it away on trifles.

Three Great Gifts Of Life

Sri Adi Shankara, the great spiritual genius of ancient India, tells us in one of his memorable works:

Jantunaam narajanma durlabham...

It is hard for any living creature to achieve birth in a human form...

It is said that upon being asked what are the greatest blessings of this world, Sri Shankara replied:

1) To be born as a human being

2) To have *mumukshatwa*, the longing for liberation, the longing for *mukti*, the yearning for emancipation from the circle of birth-death-rebirth

3) To be in contact with a *tatvadarshana* – someone who has beheld God face to face, to whom God is the greatest reality of life

In the Hindi language the same idea is expressed forcefully, yet simply: *Manush janam durlabh hai, hot na baron bar...*

Millions of species live upon this planet earth. There are micro organisms, unicellular organisms, insects, worms, flies and hundreds of other creatures of whose existence most of us are unaware. But the crown of creation, the highest order of species on earth is homo sapiens, the human being. Man is at the top of the evolutionary ladder.

This great gift of the human birth is bestowed on all of us – billions after billions of human beings, down the ages – but how many of us have realised its value?

In our ancient scriptures we are told the story of an old woman, bent double with age, walking along the road with only a stick to support her. Some men who met her on the way, asked her out of kindness and curiosity, "Mother, where are you going, all alone, on this long and lonely road?"

The old woman smiled at them – and her eyes smiled too – as she replied, "I am going to where I came from!"

Manush janam durlabh hai ...

Rare is it for any creature to achieve birth as a human being; even rarer is it to be blessed with good health and strength; and yet, what do we do with these gifts?

Alas, we devote our lives to amassing wealth; we chase after shadow-shapes of power, pleasure and possessions. Born in this world to seek our true Home, we are lost in worldly activities and are chained in bonds of worldliness!

According to the theory of transmigration, it is said that the soul passes through thousands upon thousands of lower species and forms before finally attaining the gift of the human form. So it is that Guru Arjan Dev tells us:

> For countless lives thou diverse forms didst take
> Of elephant, insect, fish or snake,
> Of horse or deer, bird or tree,
> And thus were aeons passed by thee;
> Much time in misery hast thou spent,
> Till thou a human form were lent...

Unfortunately man does not behave differently from animals. Many human beings look like humans but their behaviour is that of animals.

A wise saint tells us, "Dear one! You have received this gift of the human body; you are a human being but you limit yourself to the actions of an animal. Animals eat, drink, sleep and cohabit. Man too does much the same – he eats, drinks, sleeps and produces children. How are you different from an animal?"

You may be annoyed by this question: you may choose to argue that man is superior to animals because he is capable of doing good deeds. The answer to this would be that even animals do good deeds. Dogs often save their masters from calamities. Recently, I read in a newspaper about a dog who saved a drowning child. Such instances are many. Dogs are trained to do domestic work like picking up newspapers and bringing groceries. I read of a dog who was trained to bring bread for his master. The master only had to tie a cloth bag around his neck and the dog would go to the grocer and the shopkeeper would put the bread in the bag. One day the dog's master found four slices missing from the loaf. This happened for a few days, and the master became suspicious. So one day he followed the dog. The dog collected the bread and went into a nearby park. In the corner of the park was a blind cat who had delivered five kittens. The dog kept the bag in front of the blind cat. The cat removed four slices of bread; the dog then picked up the bag and ran to his master's house.

Think for yourself, dear friends: how did the dog know that the cat was blind? How did the dog know that the cat had delivered kittens? How is it that the dog felt like giving away a few slices of bread which belonged to his master? Nature has its own mysterious ways which we cannot fathom! Some animals are kind. They do good things instinctively. Man too does kind deeds but the difference between a man and an animal is that man often does good to satisfy his ego. Man flatters himself by his actions of kindness. He looks down upon others and prides himself on the goodness of his heart. This ego casts a shadow, a stain upon his good *karma*.

The second blessing that Sri Shankaracharya talks about is the gift of yearning. How many of us have this thirst for the Lord? How many of us make Him the goal of our life? Most of us are in slumber, for we have forgotten the purpose for which we are born. Only a chosen few have this thirst for the Lord. An awakened man focuses on his goal. But he does not shirk his worldly duties. He carries them out conscientiously. Such a man is *in* this world; but he is not *of* the world; he is not worldly. We too should realise that this human life has been given to us for a higher purpose; we should struggle against our lower self, and attain to God; for without struggle there can be no victory.

The third gift that Adi Shankara mentions is the company of saints and sages. The saints are realised souls who are actually *muktas* – liberated ones, who dwell here amongst us only to lead us across to the other shore. They know the obstacles on this path. They know the temptations which obstruct the way. With their wisdom and insight, they can guide us and help us overcome the obstacles to Liberation.

There was a *dervish* who was born in Iran. He urged his disciples to have a vision of the Lord every day. "The day you do not get to see His vision is a wasted day," he would tell his followers. The disciples said to him, "Alas, *huzoor*! We do not have the eyes to see the vision of God." The saint replied, "If your eyes cannot give you the vision of the Lord, then you must see those who have already had the vision. Therefore, be close to those who have seen the Light. Serve them and the day will come when you too will have a glimpse of that vision."

Unfortunately we do not put into practice the teachings of saints and sages. I know some people who go to a doctor and get medicines prescribed for themselves when they fall ill; but they do not bother to take those medicines! Very often this is done out of sheer laziness or forgetfulness. Just by getting the prescription to cure the disease, the disease cannot be cured. Similarly, if we listen studiously to the guidance of saints, but fail to act according to their advice, it will not lead us anywhere.

A saint invited his disciple, who was a busy official, to come and pray with him during his daily *satsang*.

"I wish I could," said the man. "But the trouble is, Master, I am too busy at the moment!"

"You remind me of a man walking blindfold in the jungle," said the Master. "And he said he was too busy to take the blindfold off."

When the official pleaded lack of time, the Master said, "What a sad mistake it is to think that one cannot pray for lack of time!"

My friends, you find time for everything else. You attend to your business or profession. You make time for family and friends. You set aside time for parties, picnics and movies. How is it that you cannot set aside 15 minutes out of your busy schedule, to sit quietly and commune with God?

Everyone is busy making money nowadays. They think only of millions and multi-millions. But you cannot take your millions with you, when you leave this world and enter the Great Beyond – as indeed we all must, one day. That day is coming, sure as the sun rises in the east, that day is fast approaching when we will have to leave behind everything – not only all the millions we have made, but also our near and dear ones, family, friends and relatives, our positions, our possessions, our power, all that we have accumulated here. What will we carry with ourselves on that day? What will we take with us when we set out on the inevitable journey?

Association with a saint or a holy one will give you the answers to all these questions.

Very often, when I ask people why they are not attending *satsang* regularly, the reply is, "There is no time" or "I am busy with my work" or "I do not even get time to take a deep breath..." and so on. Such excuses cannot fool anyone, not even the people who make these excuses! Some people even say, "Well, when I retire from my active job, I will definitely devote my time to *satsang*, spiritual pursuits and God." But such time rarely comes.

Man's life is so crowded with mundane activities, that he rarely has time for self-study and introspection. He seldom finds himself in that expansive, tranquil mood of silence and reflection, where he can listen to God, and chant the Name Divine in the heart within.

My humble request to all of you, my fellow beings, is to spare some time for *satsang*. By all means do your work sincerely. Work is essential for a human being. It disciplines his mind and exercises his body. Work is a great boon. But we must remember, work is a means, it is not an end. Livelihood must never be confused with life. Do not make your work the objective of your life on this earth. The purpose of your life is to cultivate the soul. Hence, even while you are attending to your work, stay connected to the Source of all Life; stay in constant touch with God. If you are able to set aside personal time, spend some of that valuable time in any form of *sadhana* that appeals to you. If you give eight or nine hours a day to your work, it should not be difficult to spare one or two hours for your spiritual growth! This will help you achieve the kind of inner peace and bliss that work can never bring to you.

To be successful on the spiritual path we need four kinds of blessings. It is God, in His Divine grace, who bestows these blessings on us.

The first is to be blessed with a sound physical body. The second blessing is the knowledge of scriptures. The third is the grace of the Guru and the fourth is to be blessed with a balanced mind, which is steady, in a state of equanimity. Even if we are fortunate enough to receive the first three blessings, we would fail to make any progress on the path, if we have a drifting, wandering mind, lacking in focus.

Imagine for yourself, a child born into a family with spiritual leanings and closely connected with saints. The child who is brought up in such an environment is privileged to be blessed by holy ones. As he grows up, he would be taken to *satsang* to meet the holy ones and hear spiritual discourses. But may I say to you, none of these would have any influence on him if his mind is weak and unreceptive! He would not have the power to resist worldly temptations. He would not have the strength to resist evil and sin. He would lack the will to follow the path to Liberation.

The path of the aspirant is the path of *shreya* – tough and difficult. We need a very strong will power to walk this path. Unless our mind is firm and fixed on the goal, we cannot reach it.

Guru kripa, Shastra kripa and Ishwara kripa are essential to make us strong willed. Once the mind is made up and fixed on the goal, progress is easier to achieve.

One of the best ways to strengthen our concentration, focus and will power is to begin the day with God. Therefore, our saints and sages tell us to wake up early in the morning and chant the Name Divine.

Amrit vela sach naam
Vadiahian vichar

Wake up early in the morning and chant the Name Divine. Do not allow this sacred hour to slip away unutilised. Connect yourself with your higher self, gather your inner energies and be prepared to fight the battle of life during the day. Such a start to the day will keep you in awareness of the divine presence throughout the day, and protect you from falling a prey to temptations and losing your way.

But let me warn you, waking up at *Brahma Mahurat*, offering prayers and chanting the name divine has no meaning if it does not change your inner self; if it does not bring about a transformation within you. The whole purpose of prayer and incantation of the Name Divine is to purify oneself. The whole purpose of this *sadhana* is to bear witness to the Divine presence in deeds of daily life.

How can we do this? We must become soft-spoken, kind, gentle, tender and understanding. We must express compassion and kindness in whatever we do or say. We must stop being judgmental. We must not criticise others. We must stop complaining and start thanking the Lord. Once the mind is purified in this manner, it will help us in our efforts to bear witness to the truth.

Rahiman iss sansaar mein
sabse miliye daya,
Na jaane kis bhes mein
Narayan mil jaye

Let us take this thought with us today: we must realise the value of this human birth, practise silence, experience our divinity in thought, word and deed. We must create the kingdom of Krishna where the river of love flows perennially, where kindness provides shade to the weak and meek, and where the radiance of divinity fills the world.

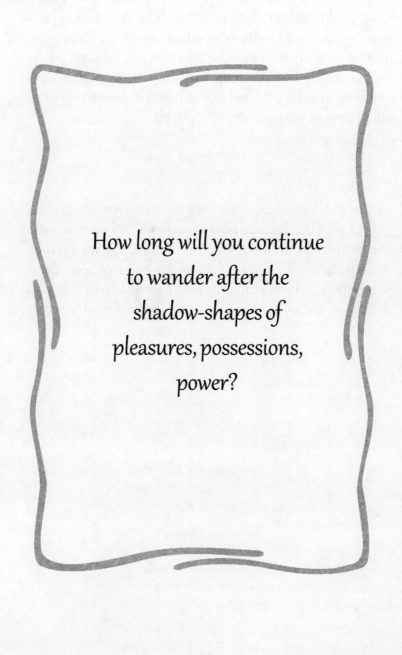

How long will you continue to wander after the shadow-shapes of pleasures, possessions, power?

The Monarch Who Became A Mystic

Today, I bring to you an invaluable lesson for life. This lesson comes to us with the blessings of a Muslim saint by the name of Bahu. Sant Bahu was at one time a great sultan. By God's grace there came about a great transformation in his life. He became a mystic; a spiritually evolved soul, who renounced all worldly power and possessions to seek the Truth of life. In one of his poetic utterances, he tells us:

> I am neither a *jogi*, nor an ascetic;
> Nor have I done penance for forty days.
> He who is asleep even when he is awake, wasting every breath,
> He is the faithless one, says my *Murshid*!

Those are intense words. They appear simple, but are difficult to grasp. How can one be said to be asleep even when he is awake? How is it possible for a man to waste every breath?

What the saint refers to is spiritual awakening – a shift in consciousness that enables us to rise beyond the level of material existence and experience the truth of our being – the truth of the *atman*. Whatever we say and do outside this awareness, whatever we say and do in identification with our narrow, physical existence, is wasted effort, in spiritual terms; which means all our efforts to please the senses, amass wealth and pursue pleasures are equivalent to dwelling in a state of sleep. Awakening from such a state into spiritual awareness does not come easily to us all. It is a great blessing bestowed upon the chosen few, who receive the grace of the Lord.

Often I am asked the question, "How may we know that we are the chosen ones? How do we realise that God's grace is upon us?"

Truly speaking, God's grace is on all of us. But it manifests itself at a particular time in our life. That is when an inner voice tells us, "This world and the life you live in are no more than illusions." Then, we become aware of the shallowness, indeed the emptiness of our pursuits and our daily activities. We realise that lasting happiness eludes us. The things we have loved and sought after, no longer interest us. We are dissatisfied, disillusioned with all that we have acquired and achieved in worldly terms. A feeling of *vairagya* – that is, dispassion, absence of desire – overtakes us. This feeling is latent in all of us. It comes to the surface, when we have passed through certain special experiences. But to some of us, it comes of its own accord, before too much time has been lost in worldly pursuits. That is because of our previous good *karmas*.

Sometime ago, I received a letter from a sister. She was what you would call a socialite. She lived the life of a social butterfly, flitting from one party circuit to another. Her rounds of parties were never ending. This had lasted for years, and then, all of a sudden, disillusionment set in. She left a grand party one night, feeling empty and frustrated. In the letter she wrote that she felt lost and lonely; her life seemed to have been wasted, and she had lost interest in the kind of activities that had filled her life until then. She found her peace, in seeking the guidance of a spiritual mentor, and under his grace, she turned to the practice of silence and meditation, which helped her to find her sense of balance.

The Light inextinguishable dwells within each one of us, but we cannot see it, for it is hidden behind veils of ignorance, veils of mind and matter. The great wall of the ego stands between us and the *Paramatman* – and we cannot see the Light Divine. It is the Guru who can destroy the wall of the ego, and lead us from darkness to light.

Why do we need the Guru? The Guru is a great cleanser, a great purifier – not merely a great teacher. Caught in the web of *maya*, caught in the snare of sensual desires and worldly pleasures, we accumulate bad *karma*, birth after birth after birth. Alas, our poor efforts are not enough to cleanse these impurities. But the Guru's grace can cleanse us and lead us towards the Divine Light of God.

The "Third Eye", the Inner Eye of the Spirit remains closed for most of us, its vision impaired by our bad *karma*. The cataract of the ego, the veils of arrogance and pride, have covered this inner eye completely.

The Guru is the 'eye' surgeon, who can restore our inner vision.

When we receive the grace of God through our Guru, we begin to devalue the material world around us. We become aware of the transitory nature of existence. This disillusion is not negative or destructive; it arises out of awareness and gradually leads to mental alertness. A feeling of *vairagya* creeps in.

When we develop this spirit of *vairagya* or detachment, the pains and pleasures of material existence cease to trouble us. We become aware of what I call the First Commandment of the Gita: "You are not this perishable body that you wear; you are the immortal *atman*!"

Identification with the body leads to the illusion that the power, pleasures and possessions of this world can make us happy. But this is not true; instead, these material possessions only keep us in bondage – the bondage of ignorance, *avidya*. Once you are freed from this illusion, you will realise the Truth of the Self and move towards God-realisation. This is the process by which we may all move from illusion to reality; from darkness to light; from death to eternity.

This is what happens to Sultan Bahu. Disillusioned with the world, Sultan Bahu renounces everything and moves out in quest. A number of questions arise in his mind. "Who am I? Why did I take birth in this world? What is the purpose of my being?" He goes out in quest of a true saint, a real *fakir*, who would guide him and provide him with the answers to his questions.

When we set out in quest of the Truth of life, the Guru reaches out to us; and with his grace, annihilates the ego; he tears away the veils of ignorance which shield us from self-realisation; he reveals our true identity to us – *Tat Twamasi!* That art Thou! It is his grace that liberates us from bondage to the circle of life and death. This gift of Grace has devolved on the Guru from God Himself – for God knows that the world is in dire need of Grace. His Presence is of course Universal; He gives us the Guru, for our individual benefit, for our personal liberation. This is why our ancient scriptures enjoin us to venerate the Guru as God.

Bahu is told that there is a true saint, a genuine mystic, who lives in a humble cottage, in a small village nearby. Sultan Bahu goes to the village, to the mystic's *kutiya*. He sends a message to the *fakir*, that one who is in quest has come to seek his guidance, and humbly requests for his *darshan*. Having sent the message, he waits patiently outside the *kutiya*. Five minutes, ten minutes, an hour passes by. Sultan Bahu waits patiently, in humility and in a spirit of total surrender.

Very often, we hear of very important people who seek an audience with spiritual elders. These VIPs are more conscious of their status than the respect and reverence that is due to a spiritual leader. They are very conscious of their time and their pending appointments. If they are asked to wait, they become restless and impatient. Such impatience is hardly conducive to a meaningful spiritual encounter! If you ever get the opportunity to visit a saint, please do not make him part of a pre-fixed schedule; don't go to him with a timetable. Let your attention be focused on him, rather than your schedule! Only then are you likely to reap any benefit from the meeting.

Alas! Many of us lack patience and resolution; we are restless and allow our minds to wander ceaselessly. We cannot rein in our worldly inclinations and desires. Arjuna tells Sri Krishna:

> For the mind is, verily, fickle, O Krishna!
> It is turbulent, strong and obstinate.
> I deem it as hard to control as the wind.
>
> **(Gita, VI:34)**

But the Lord gives us hope: It is difficult to control the mind, He admits, but it can be done.

Without doubt, O Arjuna, the mind is hard to curb and restless. But it can be curbed by constant practice (*abhayasa*) and by dispassion (*vairagya*).

Vairagya is detachment; indifference to pleasure and pain. *Vairagya* comes with the realisation that desire, which afflicts all human beings, is nothing but a kind of madness which drives us from birth to birth in the wheel of life. Desire, as the Buddha realised, is the root cause of all suffering; desire, in fact, is no better than a shadow of death!

And so, Sultan Bahu waits dispassionately, patiently outside his mentor's *kutiya*. How many of us can match this kind of patience? Leave alone wait to meet the Guru, how many of us are prepared to wait patiently at traffic signals?

It would interest you, my friends, to know that Chief Justice Chainani, who at that time was acting as Governor of Maharashtra, had come to have a *darshan* of Gurudev Sadhu Vaswani. He was on an official visit to Pune, and decided to seek the Master's blessings. He came to our Mission campus, accompanied by his security personnel and his aide de camp. Justice Chainani was to leave by the Deccan Queen. He sent a message to the Railway authorities that he would have *darshan* of Gurudev Sadhu Vaswani and then embark on his train journey. The Deccan Queen was kept waiting.

In those days, it wasn't easy to meet Sadhu Vaswani. It was not that he was tied up with official engagements! Far from it; he was often lost in contemplation and communion with the Infinite. He would lock himself up in his *kutiya*, and would not emerge for hours; his own disciples and followers would never disturb him at such times.

So it was that Justice Chainani, the Governor of Maharashtra, waited patiently outside Gurudev Sadhu Vaswani's *kutiya*. In those days, it was a rule that the Deccan Queen could not be delayed for more than 15 minutes. Justice Chainani did not leave to catch his train. He had come to meet a *tattvadarshi*; the meeting was important to him; it took precedence over his public life and private business; he decided to wait till Gurudev Sadhu Vaswani stepped out of the *kutiya*. He therefore sent a message for the Deccan Queen to leave. He postponed his return journey and waited patiently to have a '*darshan*' of Gurudev Sadhu Vaswani.

So too, Sultan Bahu waited patiently outside the *Kutiya* of the fakir. Can you guess, how long he waited? You can try; but you are bound to be way off the mark. Sultan Bahu waited outside the fakir's *kutiya*, for 3 whole days and 3 nights. He did not sleep, but stood three nights in reverence at the door of the *fakir's kutiya*.

On the fourth day, the *fakir* came out of his *kutiya*, but passed him by, without so much as casting a glance in his direction. Sultan Bahu followed him. The *fakir* walked for quite some time and then finding a quiet, peaceful place, sat down. Sultan Bahu too sat down at his feet, folding his hands in reverence. The *fakir* then looked at him, called him to his side, and embraced him, saying, "You are mine. You belong to me. You need not worry!" What more could Sultan Bahu ask for? It was a moment of celestial joy for him.

If you wish to have your inner eye opened by a realised soul, you have to put aside the "I" of the ego self! You have to be humble as ashes and dust, and patient as the flagstones on the courtyard. You have to wait for the shower of Divine Grace to fall on you when it chooses. There is no point in applying pressure or trying to use your influence in such matters. You cannot manipulate a Saint to do things to suit your convenience. Once the grace of God manifests itself in your life, and you meet your guide – be he a saint, a sage, a *fakir* or a mystic, you are practically half way to the goal of your life! The doors of heaven are open for you. You see new horizons and new universes. There is no limit to your celestial experiences. But such things are not ordered and delivered instantly! You have to have patience.

The *fakir* held him close and called his name out loudly: "Bahu". He had hardly uttered the word, when Sultan Bahu went into *samadhi*. The *fakir's* call had opened the gate to celestial bliss. And wonder of wonders, he remained immersed in the ocean of bliss, not for a few minutes, but for 3 days and 3 nights, exactly the time he had waited at the door of the *fakir*. On the fourth day, Sultan Bahu emerged out of *samadhi*. Now wherever he turned, he saw the Divine Light.

Jidar dekhta hoon udhar tu hi tu hai ....

It was a Sufi *dervish* who said: "You must meet God every day. And if you cannot meet Him, go and meet someone who has met Him and who lives in constant communion with Him. The two are not separate from each other!"

Man's heart yearns for a manifestation of God. In this *Kaliyuga*, as we wait for the final incarnation of the Lord, how can we – millions of us – find His manifestation?

Therefore, in this age of strife, disharmony and severe spiritual affliction, God has sent out amongst us, God-souls, men of God, saints and *sadhus* – in short, the true Gurus. They are here with this sacred mission: to reveal God's love to us, and to lead our erring, wandering souls back to God.

In this human birth, we cannot see God in person; but it is our good fortune that we can see the Guru, hear his *upadesh*, associate ourselves with his daily *satsang*, accept his gracious *prasad* – indeed, grasp his holy feet firmly – and through Him, God's blessings and God's grace will come to us!

Samadhi gives you the *darshan* of the Divine Light that is within us. In that Divinity, your consciousness rises above the senses, and you begin to experience God in everything. Even such an experience was accorded to Bahu through the grace of his *murshid*.

Just as a ship needs a captain, so, too, the boat of our life needs the guidance of the Guru to reach the Other Shore — or else the boat will sink in the angry waves of lust, desire and greed. In everything we do let us seek to glorify our Guru and God!

The Blessings of Guru-Bhakti

As I had told you in the earlier talk, the *fakir* had loudly spoken the word, 'Bahu' into the Sultan's ear. 'Ba' means with and 'hu' means He; He is with you; you are with Him.

Sultan Bahu's third eye is opened. He sings glories of the Lord in his mellifluous voice – like the one I quoted to you earlier:

I am neither a *jogi*, nor an ascetic;
Nor have I done penance for forty days.
He who is asleep even when he is awake, wasting every breath,
He is the faithless one, says my *Murshid*!

Sultan Bahu says he is not a *yogi*. He refers to *hatha yogis* who toughen their physical body; they can hang themselves upside down from the branch of a tree, they can sleep on a bed of nails – all their *sadhana* is directed towards training their gross physical frames and achieving unbelievable physical feats. Such practices are not for all spiritual aspirants. A disciple needs spiritual growth. He has to be on the true path, ably guided by his Master. He has to be alert, he should not be swept away by the physical miracles that would only pamper his ego and distance him from his goal!

The quest should be for God and God alone. The rest are merely obstacles in the way of progress.

Bahu who was once a Sultan becomes a Saint by the Grace of God. Sant Bahu describes the value of every human breath in his poetic verse. I am neither a *Jogi* nor an ascetic nor do I do penance. He who sleeps wasting every breath is the non-believer, so says my *Murshid*. The time lost in worldly affairs is indeed time wasted. For such a life is hollow; it is life lived on the surface. It is life ignorant of the Divine spark within each one of us.

Have you ever thought about the consumerist society we live in and the power that TV advertisements have on us and especially our children? They raise human expectations, kindling desires which lead to superfluous consumption. These desires and worldly expectations are obstacles on the path of the spirit. Unfortunately we cling to these desires and do not rest till we satisfy them.

The *Murshid* cautions us against wasting our energies; for every breath which does not remember God is wasted energy.

Once a disciple was ignited by an intense longing to have a *darshan* of his Guru. The Guru lived in his *ashram* which was far away. He started his journey on foot impelled by the desire to meet his Guru. Soon darkness descended. The man thought it was time to break his journey and take rest. He plodded on till he came up on a cottage with its light twinkling in the darkness. "This seems to be a place where I can rest," he thought. He went closer to it and found that it was an *ashram*. He knocked on the door.

The caretaker opened the door. "Can I rest here for the night?" he asked. "Why not?" the man replied, "You can come in and rest for the night". The Saint living in the *ashram* was sitting across the room. He asked the disciple, "Where are you going?" The man replied, "I am on my way to have *darshan* of my Guru, so-and-so, who lives in such-and-such a place."

Hearing these details, the saint said, "Alas! Your Guru is no more!"

The man was stunned. It was nearly ten o'clock at night. But he did not want to waste any more time. He wanted to resume his journey immediately. "I must leave now," he said. "I could not have *darshan* of the Guru when he was alive. Let me at least have his last *darshan* and his blessings. If I leave right away, I will be able to see his body." He immediately left for his Guru's *ashram*.

He walked throughout the night and reached the *ashram* in the early hours of the morning. The *ashram* was immersed in silence. There was no sign of the Guru's passing away. He knocked on the door and as soon as it was opened he eagerly asked, "Is everything alright?" "Yes, all is well," came the reply. The disciple hesitantly asked, "How is Guruji's health?" The answer was his health is perfect. Not convinced he inquired: is Guruji there? The *ashram* inmate replied, "Yes, Guruji is very much here. All the inmates of the *ashram* are meditating in the hall".

Now the disciple was puzzled. The saint at the *ashram* had said that his Guru has passed away but here everything was alright. It was a riddle he had to solve.

At last, when he met his Guru, he could not hold himself back. He narrated the incident in the saint's *ashram* to his Guru. The Guru said, "The saint was not lying to you. Last night, at about ten o'clock, I experienced negative vibrations which for a while disconnected me from God. True enough, for that period of time I was a soulless person. I was dead."

Jo dam Gafir so dam Kafir. (The breath that is empty of the memory of the Divine is the faithless one)

Friends, the moment we lose our link with God we become disconnected with the Divine Source of all life. Therefore, we should remember God all the time. Whatever work you do, remember the Name Divine. Let it be a part of your being, part of your breath.

It is difficult to put this into practice for those who work in shops, factories and offices. Even people who are involved in mind work will find it difficult to remember God. True, it may be difficult, but it is not impossible. By practice one can train the mind to remember God. If it is difficult to remember Him every moment, we can at least remember God once every hour. There are 24 hours in a day of which 8 hours go in sleep; of the remaining 16 hours if we remember God once every hour, it will be 16 times. Take hold of any verse, prayer or inspirational thought when you wake up in the morning. You may take up a verse from Shrimad Bhagavad Gita. Choose whatever is to your liking. Remember whatever you recite, it should be done with love and devotion. I recommend to my friends the simple prayer: *Deena Bandhu deena nath, meri dori Tere haath.* "O, Protector of the weak and helpless, I leave the thread of my life in Your hands. Protect me, guide me, show me the way. Take care of me." Having chanted this, you need have no fears and no worries. Keep repeating these sacred words.

Believe me, by doing so, your life will take a new turn, wonderful things will happen and you will gain peace of mind.

In the Bhagavad Gita Sri Krishna tells Arjuna: *Patram, Pushpam, Phalam, Thoyam* – a leaf, a flower, a fruit or a drop of water offered to Me with deep devotion – I accept. Whatever you do or offer at the Holy Feet of the Lord, do it with intense feeling of love and devotion. God wants from us nothing but our love. Hence kindle the fire of love within. Be awakened and you will reach the zenith of spirituality.

Once there lived a *dervish* who had two disciples. Both had the same name, Moti. One was Moti Gulabrai and the other was Moti Harchandrai. The Saint was very fond of Gulabrai. When the *dervish* felt his end was near he decided to bequeath his spiritual knowledge to his devoted disciple. He called out, "Moti, Moti", but at that moment Moti Gulabrai was not present. The other Moti went running to the *dervish* humbly and said, "Gurudev, Moti Gulabrai is not here. Moti Harchandrai presents himself in your Holy service." The *dervish* said, "You were alert; hence I bequeath all my *shakti* to you." Moti Harchandrai became the Chosen One, because he was alert, and awake. He received the grace of the *dervish*.

Guru-bhakti is for our own lasting benefit, for the Guru stands to gain nothing by it!

But the good that we derive from *Guru-bhakti* is unbelievable:

- At the highest level, it confers liberation upon us – and everlasting peace and joy, in union with God.
- As human beings, it helps us to cultivate the spirit of detachment and desirelessness to the extent that is possible for each one of us, thus freeing us from the bonds of *moha* and *maya*.

- At a lower level, constant devotion to the Guru also helps us to gain control over the lower emotions and passions, to resist dangerous temptations and to desist from wrong and sinful actions.
- In our everyday lives, *Guru-bhakti* gives us the strength to conquer fear, pessimism, despair, anxiety and negative thoughts.

The best thing is that we need no special spiritual attainment to practice *Guru-bhakti Yoga!* All we need is a yearning heart, an aspiring soul! And our role-models are great saints and holy men who have conquered the self and attained immortality through *Guru-bhakti*. Thus, we find ourselves in the brotherhood of evolved souls, when we start on the path of *Guru-bhakti*.

A Guru inspires us by his living example. He sees the potential in us that we ourselves are not aware of. He provides tremendous power of incentive and inspiration and cures us of crippling negative emotions. As the seeker proceeds on the path, he must never forget that he is always under the umbrella of his Guru.

The Guru is the great protector. But it is up to us to make full use of his protection.

You too, must be alert and awake every moment of your life. Remember God; offer prayers to Him. The prayers need not be long. A few lines, a few words will suffice.

Everyone one of us has longing, deep yearning, but the yearning is for material or physical objects. A girl longs for a boy and a boy longs for a girl. This longing becomes an obsession. Do we ever long for God as a lover yearns for his beloved? If we had such intense yearning then God himself would manifest and pour His Divine love on us.

The Sufi Saint Abu Hussan often said that God's yearning to meet His beloved devotees is far stronger and more intense than the devotee's longing for Him. God's longing for man is a thousand times greater than man's longing for God. This is very true, for God is an ocean of love. And we are only a drop of love. If you love God and long for Him, He too will love and long for you. If it rains and you hold an umbrella to protect yourself you will not get wet by the rain. God's love is like the rain. Unfortunately man holds the umbrella of worldly desires and is not able to receive the Grace of God. But if you throw away the umbrella by remembering the Lord, you will surely receive his benedictions. Make God your best friend; make Him your senior associate whenever you begin your work. Seek His support and blessings. When you are through with your allotted tasks, when you have completed the day's work, do not forget to thank Him. Above all, pray to Him for constant memory of His Name Divine; and ask to be blessed with his remembrance always.

How may we achieve such blessing and such insight in our human life? So let me pass on to you a few practical suggestions:

1. Pray to God for His special grace: He is all kindness, all compassion, He is the origin and source of all that is good and positive and wholesome. When you acknowledge that He is your Father and Mother, you live in the awareness that you are God's child and He will do only what is best for you.

2. Seek the guidance of a Guru, a spiritual mentor. Spending time in the presence of an evolved soul is the most powerful source of strength and inner wisdom. A

Guru inspires us by his living example. He sees the potential in us that we ourselves are not aware of. Above all he encourages us to believe that we are also capable of achieving what he has! He provides tremendous powers of incentive and inspiration. He cures us of crippling negative emotions. In this human birth, we cannot see God in person; but it is our good fortune that we can see the Guru, hear his words of wisdom, associate ourselves with daily *satsang*, accept his gracious *prasad* – indeed, grasp his holy feet firmly – and through Him, God's blessings and God's grace will come to us!

3. Cultivate self-discipline. The Gita teaches us that *tamas* is overcome by *rajas* – the principle of action, energy and dynamism. When we cultivate discipline of the mind, it will automatically lead us to *sattva* – light and harmony. With this enlightenment, our spiritual progress can be rapid. Offer all that you are, all that you have, all that you do, to the Lord, in a spirit of surrender – a spirit of *arpanam*.

4. Sri Krishna tells us in the Gita: "Whatever you eat, whatever you give in charity, whatever austerity you practise, whatever you do, O Arjuna, make it as an offering unto Me." This is the best antidote to conquering the ego, negating pride and arrogance. Whatever you do, offer it to God. Whatever you achieve, it is His grace, His doing. Therefore say to Him: "I am not the doer. I am but a broken instrument. If there are any shortcomings, any mistakes that I make, they are mine. But all glory belongs to Thee!"

It is your greatest good fortune to come into contact with a Guru who awakens the *atman*. It is God's grace that leads you to meet such a one on the pathways of life. You will look at him, he will look at you, he will look *into* you, he will read your heart as the pages of an open book. Each will recognise the other, and you will hear within your heart, his whisper, "Come, my child! Follow me!" And, without a single question, a single doubt, you will follow him wherever he leads you.

It is only when you have found your Guru that your spiritual journey begins, in earnest. And you do not have to leave your home and wander far and near, in search of such a One. All you need to do is: aspire, aspire!

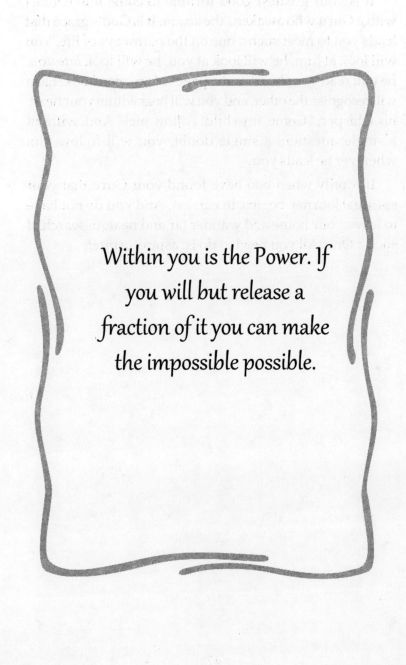

Within you is the Power. If you will but release a fraction of it you can make the impossible possible.

Awakening the Kundalini

People often ask me about integration of the mind. What is it, and how can it be achieved?

Integrating the mind simply means becoming more conscious and aware of each moment, being present during each moment; an integrated mind leads to greater insight, higher perception, intuitive wisdom – and these, in turn, make joyous and contented living possible.

The next question is invariably this: how can I learn to integrate the mind?

I know this is a difficult task. I recommend the practice of silence, which has been dear to me from a very early age; but many of my friends tell me that silence is evasive. The mind wanders and no matter how hard you try to control it, it is impossible to quieten its internal noise! I have friends who are in the habit of practising some discipline or the other everyday; but they too confess that they find it tough to still the mind, to control the stream of thoughts and to resist the desire to communicate their feelings and desires.

It is not easy to remain in a state of silence! It requires rigorous practice and self-control. And yet, I must remind you, it has been practised by our saints and sages for thousands of years! A complete teacher in itself, silence is one of the best instruments of transformation, integration, awareness and healing.

How is silence such a potent force? The answer is simple. There is a vital flow of energy that is flowing throughout the universe; the same current of life energy also flows through our body, at every moment of life. Most of this energy is spent on talking, thinking, reacting to external stimuli in our waking moments. It is, of course, dormant in our sleep. Now imagine a state of awakened consciousness, when you stop this endless stream of thought, speech and reaction. You stop responding; you stop judging what happens; you stop worrying; you stop thinking about what you should do and how you should plan for contingencies that may arise in the near or distant future. The vital energy that is saved from all these external engagements becomes a tremendous source of creative and healing power!

Within each one of us is Infinite energy. Within each one of us is a treasure of unlimited power. Unfortunately, we do not put it to right use. Instead we fritter it away on useless activities, achieving nothing worthwhile for ourselves or others. In fact, some of our activities are so negative and unfulfilling, that we often feel drained and exhausted at the end of the day, without achieving anything substantial! A weak mind troubles us and tortures us constantly; an unleashed mind runs wild and distracts us. It is only the quietened mind that can focus our life energy and enable us to transform our thought process and our life.

I repeat; the restless, wandering, distracted mind can be quietened by the primordial *shakti* within us – when this *shakti* is harnessed, made to rise above the senses, and withdrawn from responding to external distractions, when the mind is quiet and this energy is focused within, it brings with it a sense of peace which is indescribable – for it is the result of an integrated mind.

"Master, tell me in a few simple words the secret of meditation", asked a disciple.

The master said: "The secret of meditation is – quieten the mind!"

People who attempt disciplines like silence or meditation, wonder if they should try to think certain thoughts; whether they should empty the mind of all thoughts or simply let the mind drift, with its own memories and associations flowing in.

Silence should help you rise above both the dreamy subconscious and the restless conscious mind. The aim of meditation, as experts tell us, is to bring us in touch with our super conscious state. This involves three stages, as experts point out to us: relaxation, interiorisation and expansion. Let me explain the process in stages:

1) You become utterly relaxed in body and mind.

2) You focus your attention, you concentrate single-mindedly on the object of your meditation.

3) As a culmination of this process of concentration, you expand your own sense of identity, until you realise your unity with all creation, the entire universe, and with the Supreme Energy which pervades all creation and the entire universe.

Healers from alternative therapies will tell you that *prana* or breath, is itself an all-pervasive, subtle energy which is extremely potent, like electricity. One who controls his *prana* has a very powerful personality and powerful vibrations. But *prana* is only one aspect of our inner *shakti*; there is a far greater treasure of spiritual energy or *ojas shakti* within us. A spiritually evolved person can, with the help of this *shakti*, charge *prana* with great Divine Force and harness it for greater purpose.

Most of us are not aware of this primordial energy within us. This energy is invaluable. But unfortunately, in most people it is consumed by *kama*, desire or lust. This energy takes time to form and reinforce itself. But man is impelled by his basic instincts to use his energy in satisfying his sexual urges; in fact, many people focus on developing this aspect of their sexual energy rather than concentrating on their spiritual energy. Their purpose is limited: it is nothing but the pursuit of satisfying sensual desires. What they fail to understand is this: if this fantastic energy is sublimated into creative, spiritual energy, it can work wonders for us!

Let me explain to you how this energy is formed, so that you may understand how valuable it is. One hundredth of what we eat forms into a drop of blood. One hundredth of each drop of blood is converted into bone material. One hundredth of the bone tissue forms the universal element. One hundredth of this universal element forms a drop of primordial / sexual / reproductive / self-producing energy. Just think how valuable is this serpentine energy! For a momentary physical pleasure, we waste this energy. This is why our minds are not at peace.

I used the term, serpentine energy, with good reason. The Sanskrit word, *kundalini*, means coiled, like a snake. *Kundalini* energy is little understood by most people; even practitioners of yoga and meditation are not quite clear about it. However, it is mentioned extensively in Buddhist and Hindu literature, pertaining to Yoga.

Traditionally, two ways have been recommended by teachers for awakening the *shakti* within us: active and passive. The active approach involves systematic physical exercises and techniques of concentration, visualisation, *pranayama* and meditation under the guidance of a competent teacher. These techniques which are essentially based on the four main branches of *yoga*, are sometimes referred to in this connection, as *kundalini yoga*. The passive approach is perhaps allied to the path of self-realisation through surrender: here, the aspirant lets go of all the impediments to the awakening, rather than trying to actively awaken the *kundalini*.

Meher Baba, himself a spiritually awakened master, tells us that *kundalini shakti* enables man consciously to cross the lower planes and ultimately merge into the universal cosmic power of which it is a part. He adds one important point: that the awakened *kundalini* is helpful only up to a certain degree, after which it cannot ensure further progress. It cannot dispense with the need for the grace of a Perfect Master.

In India, *kundalini* energy and its awakening have been acknowledged by masters like Sri Aurobindo, Swami Paramahamsa Yoganand and Swami Sivananda. The Theosophical Society has taken *kundalini* yoga to the West, where its healing and transformative power have been acknowledged by eminent psychiatrists like Karl Jung. It must be stressed however, that in Hindu spiritual tradition, awakening this tremendous spiritual energy has been associated with cleansing the impurities in our subconscious and focusing the mind on God as a means to attain Liberation.

Friends, if you wish to control and preserve this precious energy and to put it to the highest use, you should be wary of your thoughts. Every thought has its own energy. A positive thought generates positive energy which can be tremendously uplifting and peace giving. A negative thought produces energy which is unhealthy and disturbing. An important scientific rule is this: energy follows thought. As we often say: you are what you think; you achieve what you believe in. The energy your thoughts create, accumulate and work on the universal radar!

Let me give you the story of a young girl, whose life was transformed by the power of thought. This young lady was from a rich and powerful family; she lacked nothing in terms of material wealth and comforts. But she was not what her peers and the society regarded as "pretty" or "good looking". In fact, her own family thought she was quite ugly. But as she belonged to a wealthy family, she led an active social life, filled with parties and functions and banquets. As her friends began to get married, one by one, she too wished to enter the married state. But here, her looks proved to be a great deterrent. She was turned down by eligible young men and their families, as she did not meet their conventional criteria of good looks.

Frustrated and unhappy, the girl realised the shallowness and the hollow values of the society she belonged to. Fed up with her empty life stuffed with partying and socialising, she quit her party circle and decided to devote her life to something constructive. What gave her the courage to turn her back on her superficial life was the realisation that she was a child of God; though her looks were unattractive, she was blessed with a pure and kind heart. Why should she waste her time, socialising with people who judged her superficially and went only by face value? Why not instead use her time and energy, in the service of Krishna? Once her thoughts shifted from the 'negative' energy of the party circuit, to the positive energy of service of her fellow human beings and love for the Lord, she was a changed person. She was transformed both physically and spiritually. One fine day, not long after her lifestyle change, a good, kind man who saw a soul-mate in her, proposed marriage to her.

She hesitated. She thought to herself: why would anyone want to marry an ugly duckling like me? The man said to her, "Have you seen your face in the mirror recently? Just see it." The truth was that the girl had been so oppressed by the negative feedback in the past that she had stopped viewing herself in the mirror; now, when she saw her face in the mirror, and carefully studied it, she was surprised. She looked good! The young man spoke to his parents about his choice of spouse. The 'proposal' talks were initiated, and the couple got married soon thereafter. That is the effect of thoughts on your physical, emotional and spiritual being.

Once you divert your mind to something which is positive, the stress of the negative feelings will be released, and you will find good things happening in your life miraculously. Thought power is universal. Each one of us has this power. We have to take care of our thoughts, to harness this power. Remember, thoughts are the building blocks of your destiny. Some thoughts are base and belong to the lower domain of vices and sins. We have to block the flow of such thoughts. We have to invite thoughts which belong to the higher sphere of light – thoughts of kindness, forgiveness, love and humility. Some thoughts such as those of 'kill', 'revenge', 'tit for tat', may excite us and we find pleasure and satisfaction, when we entertain them in our minds or watch them in action in stories, in print or in 'moving images' in cinema. Some of our sports are also based on 'fight to the finish'. Such thoughts harm us and others. Such thoughts have to be purified, in order to gain peace and inner stability.

As I said earlier, the 'serpent' of energy lies coiled at the base of seven subtle *chakras* in the human body. This energy is to be released and raised above the physical senses in order to integrate and to still the mind.

In ancient India the students had to practice self-control during the life stage which we refer to as the '*Brahmacharya*' stage. It was a period in which they lived a life of austerity, simplicity and abstinence from sense pleasures. Today, many teenagers and college students go to college just to have fun. Students of the opposite sex, girls and boys, mingle freely. Swept away as they are by western ideas of fun and freedom, they adopt a permissive life style, which encourages sensual indulgence. This results in loss of the primordial energy. If you live only on the physical level, your mind is bound to roam around the pleasure haunts – leaving joy, peace and wisdom far behind.

Therefore, young people should avoid thoughts of lust, desire, and indulgence. They must remind themselves constantly: "I am not this body that I wear; I am the immortal *atman*." For let us remember, every one of us is spiritual and carries the Divine spark within. Let us purify our thoughts; let us remain calm; act with detachment and watch what moves through our minds. We have to practice self-control. We have not only to safeguard the '*shakti*' within, but we have to regenerate it, gather it, give it a force which would elevate it above the gross physical. We must control lustful impulses. Lustful impulses are also expressed in anger, in revenge, in quarrel and futile fights.

It is when we get rid of vicious thoughts and desires of the 'lower domain' that we will be able to build the 'pure primordial' energy.

Some people are so entrenched in basic desires that even death cannot pull them out – unable to pull themselves away, they hang about on earth as 'disembodied' spirits.

A man had married four times. On his death bed, he held his youngest wife's hand and passed away. The wife then went through the nightmare of a spirit visiting her constantly and holding her hand!

Your vital energy and its regeneration also depends upon the type of food you take. *Satvic* food – pure vegetarian diet – is best for you. Flesh diet – the cooked remnants of carcasses – pollute our insides, thus creating obstacles in the process of energy regeneration. Also try to eat less. For the more you fill your stomach, the more lazy and sleepy you will feel. In order to still the mind and to meditate, it is essential that your stomach is not clogged with food, or else all your energy will be spent digesting the food.

Gurudev Sadhu Vaswani said: Cultivate the Soul. Purify your mind. Detach yourself from the shadows. Be awake; open your eyes. Rise above the senses and do not be led away by illusionary pleasures. Let us offer a prayer to the Lord:

> Lord, purify me. Cleanse me.
> Make me gentle, make me fair and just and true.

Prayer has the power to unleash and regenerate the primordial energy. Awaken this Divine power within you and put it to the best possible use. Realise your Divine potential!

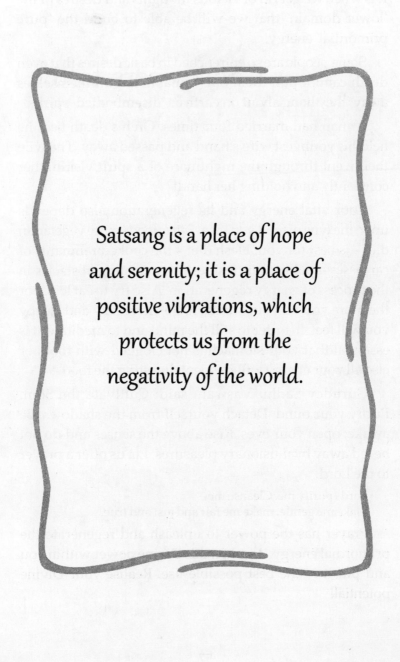

Satsang is a place of hope and serenity; it is a place of positive vibrations, which protects us from the negativity of the world.

The Four Gatekeepers to the Kingdom of God

There is a saying in English, "Birds of a feather, flock together". That may be the case with birds; as humans, we can always choose our friends. They can be like-minded, or they can be very different from us; but the point is that their company and association must help to make us better human beings! So it was a wise man who said, "Tell me the company you keep, and I will tell you what kind of a person you are."

I would certainly agree with that view. If your company, the friends you keep, your associates are good, your life will be good too! We know one drop of lemon juice or any acidic substance can curdle a whole can of milk; one rotten apple in a basket will spoil the other apples. One wrong friend is enough to lead you astray - if you let him! That is why we are told from childhood that we should choose our friends carefully. We should avoid undesirable people and keep the company of pure, holy and cultured friends.

Guru Nanak Dev, himself a beacon of hope and spiritual guide to thousands in his lifetime, tells us in his *bani*:

Jun Nanak Dhoorr Mungai Tis Gurasikh Kee
Jo Aap Jupai Avureh Naam Japaavay

Servant Nanak begs for the dust of the feet of that Gurusikh, who himself chants the *Naam*, and inspires others to chant it.

Kunti's eldest son, Suryaputra, Karna (son of the Sun God) was born with the sacred *kavach* and *kundal* (armour and ear rings) bestowed on him by his illustrious father. He was endowed with all the good qualities of his father. As we all know, he was the very embodiment of generosity and the true spirit of giving. Like the sun, he gave away all he had, freely and generously, asking for nothing in return. Known and revered for his *daan* and *dharma*, he even gave away the fruits or good effects of all his generosity at the point of his death, when the Lord approached him in the guise of an old brahmin seeking alms. Such was Karna's greatness and goodness. A noble soul, a brave warrior, a charitable being, he suffered a sad fate because of the company he chose to keep: he was the sworn friend of Duryodhana and the Kaurava brothers, indeed, a favourite of their evil, scheming Uncle Shakuni; and this association ruined him utterly. He fought against his own brothers, antagonised his own mother and was killed ignominiously on the battlefield of Kurukshetra!

Karna had a choice before him: when his mother revealed his true identity and begged him to join the Pandavas, he could have chosen to stay away from the doomed war: but the pull of association proved to be too strong, and so, out of a sense of misplaced loyalty and friendship, this good man gave up his life to defend the unrighteous and unjust Kaurava clan.

Modern psychology avers that we all have a conscious and a subconscious mind. Hindu philosophy has long recognised this and described the subconscious mind as the storehouse of *vasanas* or traces of the impulses and desires of previous births, countless ones at that! These desires are hidden in the subconscious mind, and they have long been suppressed; but given an opportunity they erupt like a volcano, and submerge us in the burning lava of impulsive desires.

Sant Bilwamangal was born in a family of pious folk. But he neglected his duties and responsibility to his family, and misled by the company he kept, poured all his love, affection and considerable wealth at the feet of a courtesan. But Bilwamangal was truly blessed; the courtesan was a woman who understood the truth of existence; she chided her besotted lover and said to him, "If only you bestowed on the Lord even one thousandth of the passion you have for me, you will surely gain liberation!" Bilwamangal's life was transformed! He became a *bhakta* of the Lord and his collection of songs, *Krishna Karnamrita*, was hailed as a work of ardent devotion by Sri Chaitanya Mahaprabhu. Blessed was Bilwamangal, that even among the wrong company he kept, he found one true friend who brought him back to good sense, right thinking and on to the right path!

In the early days of the Indian Independence Movement, Gurudev Sadhu Vaswani had initiated the Satyagraha Movement in Karachi. During a social protest, he and his followers were arrested and put in jail. I am happy to say that I was in Gurudev's distinguished company! In those days, it was a matter of pride and self respect for patriotic Indians to court arrest and spend a few days behind bars; they considered it a very small price to pay for the cause of freedom. And in those days, the most distinguished of our freedom fighters had a jail record. Why, Lokmanya Tilak's outstanding works were written in jail, as were the memorable books by Jawaharlal Nehru and other great leaders!

Thus it was with a sense of national pride and dedication to the cause that we entered the jail with our Gurudev. The Karachi jail superintendent at that time was one Mr. Cooper. While he was on his daily rounds he saw us locked behind the bars in a dark, narrow cell. He was very upset, that we had been given such a tiny dark cell. He reproached the jail staff and pulled them up for what he considered to be their indiscriminate attitude. "These people are not common criminals," he scolded them, "They are not like other convicts; they will not run away; please open the cell and let them move around freely."

The atmosphere in the narrow cell had indeed been stifling and we were happy to move around the jail complex and meet our fellow prisoners. True, some of them were hard-core criminals but Gurudev Sadhu Vaswani was, as ever, the soul of kindness and compassion. To him, all the so-called criminals were fellow human beings, children of the One God. He met all the convicts lovingly, spoke to them and blessed them.

I cannot tell you how happy the prisoners were to have a holy man in their midst! They flocked to him to narrate the stories of their unfortunate lives and crimes; some of them shed bitter tears of repentance and begged him to beseech God to forgive them. "We are lost souls, Dada," they said to him with tears in their eyes, "But if you bless us, we are sure that even God will forgive us!"

I still remember how distraught they were on the day of our release. They said that the whole atmosphere of the prison had been transformed by the presence of a saint amongst them; they begged Gurudev Sadhu Vaswani to remember them in his prayers, and gave us a tearful farewell.

Such is the grace of a saint that it can transform a prison into a *satsang*!

The *Yoga Vashishta* written by Maharishi Valmiki is not well known among many of us. But it is a unique work, a work of wisdom incorporating Sage Vashishta's teachings to Sri Rama, in the form of a dialogue. For countless centuries it has inspired and guided spiritual seekers. In this brilliant treatise, Sage Vashishta describes *moksha* or Liberation as a mansion with four gates, each one guarded by a gate keeper or sentry.

Who are these gatekeepers? *Satsanga, samattva, santosha and vichara* – good association, equanimity, contentment and spiritual reflection – these are described as the four "gatekeepers" of *mukti* or liberation in the Yoga Vashishta. They are also dynamic aids, we are told, in the cultivation of *saatvic* or pure living.

Friends, *satsang* is indeed a door to heaven for souls who seek the Lord's grace in this age of Kali! True happiness – the bliss of *sat chit ananda* is to be found in the heavenly abode. *Satsang* can indeed help you to get an entry into these portals of peace and happiness. For the angels themselves visit places where there are pure and holy vibrations. These angels register your presence and your absence in the *satsang*. It is not for nothing that worried, anxious, stressed people, who come to *satsang* as a matter of routine, always find themselves feeling so much lighter and better when they leave!

Once, when I attended a *satsang* at Ahmedabad, I saw that all the devotees had to wash their feet under the running water, before they entered the holy precincts of the *satsang* hall. This is a deeply symbolic gesture that Hindus adopt in many of their places of worship. It actually means that we cleanse ourselves of our worldly desires and enter the *satsang* with a clean and pure heart. We should all cultivate detachment from the desires that haunt us, at least for half an hour when we attend a *satsang*, and use that time in meditation at the Lotus Feet of the Lord.

Friends, instant happiness can be found in *satsang*, provided we are in tune, mentally and spiritually, with its invigorating vibrations. You will understand that I refer to people who are mentally and physically present at the *satsang*! Not those who simply come to mark attendance there!

The *satsang* is illumined by the radiant presence of the *Satguru*, the true Master. In this human birth, we cannot see God in person; but it is our good fortune that we can see the Guru, hear his *upadesh*, associate ourselves with his daily *satsang*, accept his gracious *prasad* – indeed, grasp his holy feet firmly – and through him, God's blessings and God's grace will come to us! Several great *bhaktas*, devout disciples of the Hindu faith, look upon their Guru's *satsang* as their temple and place of pilgrimage, not finding it necessary to seek God elsewhere.

Consider what the Guru does for us: ceaselessly he toils to take us Godward; this is the very purpose of his *upadesh*; tirelessly he gives us his sacred *upadesh*, that we might hear and reap the benefit of his grace and wisdom.

Once, they put this question to Adi Shankara: What is *Amrita* (Divine Nectar) to the ears? His reply was indeed significant: *Sadupadesha* – i.e. the good upadesh given by the Guru.

How magnanimous, how benevolent is he who offers us this nectar again and again, for our benefit! Is it not true that as we sit in the *satsang* and the nectar of the Guru's *upadesh* flows into our ears, we feel uplifted, transported, as if we are in a different world, living on a higher plane as it were? For many of us this may be a fleeting experience out of which we emerge, when we leave the *satsang* and the Guru's presence. Nevertheless, we have tasted the nectar; we have experienced the bliss; and consciously or unconsciously we want more! So we go back to the Guru and his *satsang*, again and again. And he is ever willing to pour this Divine Nectar into our ears, until we are ready to understand that this bliss is our rightful goal and destination. To this end, the Guru toils ceaselessly, tirelessly.

What have we ever done to deserve such grace, such blessing?

The answer is probably, "Nothing much!" It is the Guru's grace, rather than our deserving, that he showers this great blessing upon us. Is this not cause for the utmost gratitude and devotion to the Guru?

The Guru is constantly called upon to move from place to place: his disciples constantly seek his grace and blessings. Why should he devote his heart and soul, time, effort and energy for the welfare of us all, when he can devote himself to contemplation and meditation? What right do we have upon his time and effort? Do we even deserve his grace and generosity? Are we at least fit and ready to receive his blessings, which we crave off and on?

Gurudev Sadhu Vaswani founded the *Sakhi Satsang* in Hyderabad-Sind in 1929, and later, he formed the Brotherhood Association with the goal of affording opportunities to some to cultivate the soul. The hundreds of brothers and sisters who flocked to join his spiritual gatherings, gradually became regular *satsangis*. To this day, as many of you know, the *satsang* remains the pivot around which all the Mission activities revolve. Everyday, three *satsang* sessions are held at the Mission Campus, and people make it a point not to miss the daily *satsangs*. I am told that some of our Sadhu Vaswani Centres overseas, also hold weekly/ bi-weekly/daily *satsangs*, which also attract several of their regular participants.

This is not just my personal opinion. Many *satsangis* tell me, that *satsang* gives them a sense of stability, a positive frame of mind, a certain sense of mental well-being and peace of mind. They say that *satsang* links them with a Higher energy and in that positive, joyful atmosphere they feel happy and rejuvenated. Whether they hear discourses or recite prayers or read from the *bani* of great ones or participate in singing the Name Divine, they feel elevated. At such times, their minds are free from worldly cares and anxieties; and there awakens a desire within them, the desire to follow in the footsteps of the truly great ones. They yearn to imbibe the ideals of saints and sages, and make their life more meaningful, more worthwhile.

Satsang has a positive effect on man. *Satsang* creates pure and positive vibrations which neutralise the negative emotions of man. When we go to *satsang*, we get to hear discourses of holy men, participate in the recitation of sacred scriptures and singing of soulful *bhajans*. All of this helps to raise our levels of positive vibrations and energises us. For a short time at least, we forget our mundane worries and get immersed in the pure waters of the Spirit. Our emotions rise above the senses, and we cry out, "O Lord! This is true bliss. O Lord! You have given me this beautiful gift of life. Till now I have wasted it. But from now onwards, I will strive to achieve the goal of this human birth!"

May we all be blessed by reaping the benefits of *satsang* which gives an instant feeling of peace, inner joy and well-being.

The Name of God is the potent pill that cures all ills. By chanting the Name Divine our *antah-karan* — (inner instrument) gets purified, it draws our senses to a focus and we feel refreshed.

A Thief Called Temptation

Let us begin our reflections today with Kabir *vani*. The couplet I have chosen is :

Kabir Maya Chortey Muss Muss Lavey Haat
Ik Kabira Na Musye, Jin Kitey Bhara Paat.

Sant Kabir in this beautiful *doha*, compares the worldly temptations to a thief. The temptation breaks the man into pieces by making him succumb to base desires. No one can escape this tragedy, the only One who has escaped it is Kabir himself. For Kabir has pounded the temptations into pieces and thrown them out of his life!

How is temptation a thief? What does it steal from us?

Sant Kabir has referred to worldly temptations by many different names. In this couplet he has called temptation a thief. In other *dohas* (couplets) he has compared temptation to a poisonous snake. Everyday this poisonous snake strikes you with its deadly venom; day-by-day it weakens you, sucking your vital energy, till a day comes when you become lifeless. It has robbed you of your precious life breath. Unfortunately we do not realize it and remain under the illusion that we are enjoying life.

Friends, if only we would realise the truth that we have passed through many cycles of birth and death! For us, every birth, every life is like a shopping spree. We are tempted to buy, buy and buy more; our one desire is acquisition and possession. Our temptations force us to acquire this and possess that till our life becomes empty of its real purpose. Spending, buying, acquiring, possessing, we are slowly reduced to becoming spiritual paupers! Each birth, each life tempts us with possessions to which we get attached and hence we are robbed of the true goal of life. Instead of being focused on our ultimate Liberation, we wander after temptations and illusions which are available in plenty in the *bazaar* that is this world!

Just as thirsty wanderers in a desert run after a mirage to quench their deadly thirst, we run after worldly temptations. When we listen to the wisdom of the saints, we are brought back to our senses; we realise the true goal of life, and guard against those temptations that rob us and plunder us of the wealth of the spirit!

In his life Sant Kabir also had faced worldly temptations; but being a man of God, he did not allow it to overpower his life's goal. As Kabir says, it was by the grace of his Guru that he could avoid such temptations.

How does one get the strength to avoid the temptations of life? This inner strength comes from *Guru-Bhakti* (devotion to Guru). Sant Kabir says that he derived the spiritual strength from the *mantra* – *Ram Naam* - bestowed on him by his Guru. It is by chanting *Ram Naam* that Kabir could avoid the temptations of life and devote himself fully to the attainment of self-realisation.

Millions get trapped by temptations. People lose their vital life energy in running after illusory power, fame, prestige, money and connections.

We are all familiar with the story of Yayati. Let me narrate to you a modern parable based on the legendary king.

Yayati had lived a hundred years; he had a hundred sons; and yet, when death came calling at his door, he was not prepared to let go of life! "Spare me," he begged of death. "Spare me for a little while longer! Many, very many are the unfulfilled desires that haunt me! Let me live to satisfy at least a few of them."

"You have lived here upon this earth for a hundred years, and yet you are not satisfied!" said Death. "How much longer do you need before you are ready to give up your life?"

"A hundred years more!" pleaded Yayati, now distraught. "There is so much more that I want, so much more that I crave! How can you take me away so cruelly, leaving me no tomorrow to look forward to?"

Death was taken aback. "I have come here to take a life away; I cannot return empty handed. If you will not go with me, give me someone to take your place."

"That is easily done," said Yayati eagerly. "I have a hundred sons. One of them will surely take my place. Indeed, they have all told me several times that they will ever be willing to lay down their lives for me!"

Forthwith the hundred sons were summoned; their father's wish was explained to them; one among them was required to die so that his father could live on.

The sons were aged from twenty to seventy-five. The seventy and sixty years old were unwilling to die; those in their fifties and forties claimed they had responsibilities to fulfill; it was only the youngest of them all, barely twenty years of age, who came forward to take his father's place.

"You are crazy!" his brothers said to him. "Why, you know nothing of life! You cannot throw away your youth and joy for an old man's whim! Take back your offer. Death is cruel; and for someone as young as you, death is a tragedy."

But, in reality, death was far from cruel. It is not for nothing that Hindu belief looks upon death as Yama Raja. Yama took the young man aside and said to him, "I suggest that you reconsider your offer. You are too young to die. Look at your father. He is one hundred years old and unwilling to die..."

"Precisely," said the young man. "He has lived a hundred years and he is still unsatisfied, unfulfilled. Does that not reveal the futility of this life? And if it was only my father who felt this way, I would have thought that he was an exception. But each and every one of my brothers, at seventy-five, seventy, sixty-five and sixty years, feels the same way! They are princes; they have had the best of everything; and still they are unsatisfied. Therefore one thing is clear to me. This life is not going to be a source of contentment or satisfaction to me, however long I may live. Therefore I say to you Sir, I am ready to go with you – not in despair or ignorance, but in the full understanding that I would rather not pass through this long and futile existence only to arrive at the end unwillingly. Here I am, in full possession of my faculties and in good understanding of the meaning of worldly life. Take me, I am content to go with you."

Death relented and said to Yayati: "Your son shall be restored to youth and life when you are ready to die."

Do you know when that came to pass? It was after one thousand years! For one thousand years more, Yayati continued to live and indulge himself in as many sensual pleasures as he could. After one thousand years of worldly life, wisdom dawned on him. He recalled the words of the *Smriti:* "Desire is never extinguished by enjoyment of desired objects; it only grows stronger like the fire fed with clarified butter."

Death brought back Puru, the youngest son. Yayati embraced him and said to him, "Dearest son, sensual desire is never quenched by indulgence any more than fire is by pouring *ghee* in it. I had heard and read this, but till now I had not realised it."

Desire, according to the Buddha, is the root cause of all suffering upon this earth. And the human heart is home to a hundred thousand desires! All kinds of desires arise ceaselessly in the human heart. If the heart is strong and pure it will overcome these desires, but if the heart is impure it will succumb to the evil designs of the devil. That is why the first thing we must do is to purify the heart and the mind.

Today the emphasis is on the development of the mind. But what is the use of this mental development if the mind becomes a home of Satan? Of what use is fame and name and the material progress that we crave if our hearts are empty and wanting? Sant Kabir urges us to keep the heart pure! Do not allow demonic thoughts to ruin your life, he urges us.

Friends, reflect upon your life! As a child you were so innocent, but as you grew up, you got engulfed by worldly temptations. Gradually you lost your innocence and your loving heart. With the years you became hardened and subject to a thousand temptations.

Let us always be aware and alert, never to fall into temptations. Let the world go on. Let the illusions multiply.

Keep yourself away from the shifting patterns, the moving kaleidoscopic colours of *maya*. Do not be dazzled. These are false glitters with which the world lures you. Let them not blind you and rob you of your true light.

Once there was a gallant warrior. He started on a long journey by ship. Someone had told him about a fort which was on the other side of the ocean. In the fort was locked up a veritable treasure – a Golden Blanket. The fort was guarded by demons; no one could dare to enter the fort. The valiant soldier took up the challenge to enter the fort and get the Golden Blanket. He took a vow that he would fight the demons and find his way to the inner chamber and get the Golden Blanket.

After a few days of voyage the ship halted at a port. The warrior felt like getting down on to dry land. So he disembarked and strolled through the streets of the port. As he was walking, he heard a sweet melodious voice of a woman singing a heart-wrenching song. He was drawn by her sweet voice and his steps moved towards her house. He stepped into the house and found a beautiful woman singing. He was so enchanted by her beauty and by her singing, that he quite forgot that he had to go back to the ship. The beautiful woman charmed him by inviting him inside her chamber. He forgot all about the Fort and the Golden Blanket. He continued to live there. Years rolled on; many ships came that way but the warrior soldier continued to stay with this charming woman. He was besotted by her charm, and left his mission unfulfilled.

The worldly temptations come to us in different forms; we run after power, fame, glory, influence and success; the temptations put us into the cycle of *karma*. What is *karma*? True *karma* means to break the chain of cause and effect, to realise the self and to be in union with the Supreme Being. Unfortunately our whole life is spent in multiplying the cycle of this cause -and -effect wheel of birth and death. Our whole life is dictated by pride and ego which can only generate negative *karma*.

Friends, Sri Krishna tells Arjuna that we cannot avoid *karma*; let us do our *karma*, but let us, as the Lord suggests, surrender the fruits of all our actions to Him. When we surrender our actions to Him, *karma* cannot touch us withy its negative effects. But when all our actions are done to flatter the ego, our lives become barren. Love, kindness, devotion and service have little or no place in our agenda of action.

Sant Kabir tells us the same thing: Do not get entangled in the web of *karma*. Do your work but do it without any expectation of reward. Surrender the fruits of your action to God.

Let us reflect once again on Kabir's *doha*: Temptations are thieves and drag us into the web of *karma*, leaving us no time for chanting the Name Divine. We are so engrossed in running after the material trinkets of life that we forget our true wealth, purpose and goal on this earth plane.

In another of his *dohas*, Sant Kabir says:

Aap Tey Nagar, Aap Tey Bhandiya
Aap Tey Moah, Aap Tey Phandia!

With our effort and action the towns and cities are built; but when our actions are filled with ego, we have big cities, more people, more business, more commerce, more selfishness and more attachments!

Man does work for progress but that very progress obstructs his path to a better and a higher life! Work selflessly in the service of humanity without any expectation of the fruits of your action.

I close with the wise words of Kabir:

Kaatey Nahi Kati, Tut Nahi Jaiy,
Saap Sapan Na Hoey, Jug Ko Khaay

No matter how much we try to break this *karmic* cycle we get more and more entangled by worldly affairs. Only the grace of God and the Guru can save us from this endless cycle of temptation-desire-indulgence and frustration. Hence let us do our work but keep chanting the *Ram Naam Mantra* or the Name Divine.

Let us chant the Name Divine and be blessed!

O foolish one!
Do you not know that
desire leadeth to wreckage
and ruin, that pleasure
giveth rise to pain, that he
who seeks sensation only
suffering doth gain?
Arise, awake, and walk not
the way of pleasure but the
path of duty!

The Transformation of Francis

The *Sukhmani Sahib* is regarded by many as a unique scripture which when recited fills the heart with wondrous sense of peace. In one of its verses we have the following words:

> Phirat Phirat Prabh Aaiya,
> Pariya Tau Sharnai
> Nanak ki Prabh Venati
> Apni Bhakti Lai.

An English translation says,

> After wandering far and wide, O Lord,
> I have come and surrendered to Thee.
> This is my plea, O Nanak,
> Grant me devotion for Thy Lotus Feet!

It is, indeed, a great gift to humanity from Guru Arjan Dev. In the *Sukhmani Sahib*, every word is sacred, every word is a blessing, for it has been illumined by a saint with a universal vision.

The verse I have quoted describes the condition of many of us. We wander all our lives and exhausted by our wanderings, seek a place of refuge. We go through many trials and tribulations; our bonds and attachments only tie us down and bring misery into our lives. The world around us seems dark, and the light of love does not shine in our hearts. Indeed, love has taken a back seat in our lives. Money has built fences between brothers and sisters; property has become a bone of contention between the family members. Our joys and sorrows are weighed by the scale of money. All relationships are selfish and self-centered. The spirit of sacrifice has vanished from our lives. Living under such worldly conditions, our soul cries:

> O Lord, long have I wandered, long have I roamed,
> Tired, I rest at Your door, O Nanak, pray, bless me with *bhakti* for You...

The soul cries out in anguish because it has awakened to the One Reality of life; the awakening comes with the grace of a saint or a Guru. Many a time, when we are disillusioned by the false appearances of this world, we turn our face to God; we return to Him, but only for a while. The pull of the dark, stormy waters of desire are so strong, that we are dragged into the swirling whirlpool of unhappiness again and again.

Sufi saints have described the three journeys of life. The first journey is the one through which we are passing now! This journey takes us away from the Divine into the murky waters of the gross material world, the deep and dangerous *sansar sagar*. During this journey the mind is restless; selfishness holds us in its powerful grip; desires and worldly ambitions dominate our thoughts; the distance between me and you increases. Greed and competition become the hallmark of our existence, and our hearts become arid and drained of all energy and vitality.

Each one of us here is a pilgrim. We are travellers on a journey which often becomes difficult and depressing. To make this journey worthwhile, to make it a joyful experience, we have a simple remedy: utterance of the Name Divine. Keep chanting His Name till it permeates deep into your subconscious mind; so that even when you are working or doing domestic chores, the incantation continues automatically, without any effort. It becomes a part of your being.

Be awakened! Realise that life is only a journey, and that you have to return to your native land. Return, return, O soul! The sooner you do so, the better, for this journey is fraught with dangers. The earlier you get it over with, the better.

There is a story told to us in our ancient legends. It is, in fact, an allegory which draws a parallel between the world of *maya* and a beautiful woman.

Sri Krishna had a friend by the name of Mohan. One day, Sri Krishna and Mohan climbed up a steep hill, talking of many matters. The hill happened to be quite steep, and Sri Krishna felt very thirsty. He requested Mohan to go and fetch some water for him. Mohan went to look for water, and the very first cottage, whose door he knocked on, was opened by a beautiful woman. Mohan stared at the woman in awe. Her beauty was bewitching. Mohan was stunned by her enchanting looks. He remained rooted to the ground, staring into those beautiful liquid eyes. He dimly heard his mind's voice: "O Mohan, what are you waiting for? Get some water for Sri Krishna. He is thirsty and waiting for you impatiently!"

Mohan ignored the small, still voice; he forgot the purpose of his visit. He looked into the beautiful eyes of the girl and asked, "What is your name, O, beautiful one?"

"Madhu," the girl replied softly, staring back at him. He remained rooted to the doorstep, enamored by her beauty. The Divine Lord, his dearest friend, waited for him, thirsty and tired. But he was lost to the world!

Our condition is no better. We forget our goal when enticed by the illusory glamour of this world! This condition cannot last long; for sooner or later we realise that we have to return to our native land!

> O Traveller! Return to your Real home.
> Stop wandering.

This realisation comes with an awakening within. It makes us shed tears of repentance for having gone astray, for having lost our way Godward...When we take this U Turn, we begin our second journey upon this earth, according to the Sufi saints.

Let me add, it is not only ordinary mortals like us who are distracted by the world and its allurements. This distraction has also led great saints and devout men and women away from their path. This also happened to one of the greatest saints of the Catholic church, St. Francis.

Francis was the son of a rich cloth merchant, Pietro di Bernardone, and his wife Pica, a devout woman. His father was in France on business when Francis was born in Assisi, and Pica had him baptized as Giovanni after Saint John the Baptist (Giovanni being Italian for John); it was her wish that her son should grow up to be a great spiritual leader. However, when her husband returned to Assisi, he was furious about this, for he did not want his son to be a man of the Church. He decided to call him Francesco, in honour of his commercial success and enthusiasm for all things French. In a sense, Francis's life reflected both their aspirations!

Francis, in his youth, led a life of pleasure and comfort. He was fond of the good life, especially fashionable clothes. He nourished literary ambitions, and was rather keen on writing romantic poetry in French. His father paid him a handsome allowance, and he lacked nothing. He loved the company of his rich young friends, with whom he would roam the streets, having fun, indulging in all the pleasures and vanities of youth.

No one loved pleasure more than Francis, we are told; he had a ready wit, sang merrily, delighted in fine clothes and showy display. Handsome, gay, gallant and courteous, he soon became the prime favourite among the young nobles of Assisi, the foremost in every feat of arms, the leader of the civil revels, the very king of frolic.

He was often delegated to oversee his father's flourishing cloth business. It is said that one day, as he was engaged in selling expensive fabric to his customers, he was accosted by a beggar, who pleaded for alms. Francis was at that time about to conclude a deal for several bales of velvet, and could not leave his customers. But when the deal was concluded, he ran after the beggar, and emptied all the money in his pockets into the poor man's begging bowl. His friends chided him and made fun of him, for this unprecedented act of 'charity'. As for his father, he was enraged to hear of his son's needless generosity.

In the year 1201, when he was barely twenty, he joined a military expedition to fight a war, and was taken prisoner by the enemy state of Perugia. His stint in prison afforded him the opportunity for reflection on his future. But when he was released, he came back to Assisi and resumed his life of pleasure.

When God wants to draw someone close to Him, He finds ways and means to achieve this end. In 1204, Francis was afflicted with a serious illness, which brought about a spiritual reawakening. Perhaps he was able to perceive the emptiness, the hollowness of the life he had been leading until then!

Be that as it may, Francis enlisted to fight yet another war, seriously considering a military career for the rest of his life. On the eve of his departure, he had a strange dream, in which he saw a vast hall hung with several coats of armour, all marked with the Cross. "These," said a voice, "are for you and your soldiers."

"I know I shall be a great prince," exclaimed Francis exultingly, as he set out to fight another war. He took the dream to be an omen of a great career as a knight; but though he pursued this dream for a while, his growing spiritual yearning would not let him continue his worldly pursuits. Facing a mental crisis, he returned to Assisi, a changed man. It was now impossible for him to live the thoughtless life of his youth. He no longer enjoyed the sports and the feasts of his former companions. Puzzled by this change, they asked him mockingly, whether he was smitten by love, and was on the verge of marrying. To this, he answered "Yes, a fairer bride than any of you have ever seen!" His companions did not realise then, that his chosen 'bride' was Poverty, which he was about to embrace willingly!

Francis now began to spend much of his time in solitude and silence. He began to seek in prayer and solitude the answer to his call; he had already given up his gay attire and wasteful ways. One day, while crossing a deserted plain on horseback, Francis unexpectedly encountered a poor leper. The sight of the disfigured man, covered with the oozing sores so typical of the dreaded disease, filled him with revulsion and disgust. His first impulse was to retreat from the man; but controlling his natural aversion with a tremendous effort, he dismounted, embraced the leper and gave him all the money he had.

About this time, Francis made a pilgrimage to Rome. Pained at the meager offering of a few small coins left at the tomb of St. Peter, he emptied his whole purse there. Then, as if in rejection of his wealthy lifestyle and fussy habits, he exchanged clothes with a tattered beggar and stood for the rest of the day fasting among the hordes of beggars at the door of the famous Basilica.

On his return to Assisi, he also took to visiting the leper asylum in the town, where he nursed and cared for the stricken lepers, ostracized and abandoned by society. When they went out to beg, he begged for alms too, to support them. He would often go to pray at the Church of San Damiano, just outside of Assisi, to ask God for guidance and enlightenment. It was here that he had a mystical vision of Christ, in which the Icon of crucified Christ came alive and said to him three times, "Francis, Francis, Francis, go and repair my house which, as you can see, is falling into ruins." He thought this to mean the ruined church in which he was presently praying, and so he sold his horse and some cloth from his father's store, to assist the local priest with the repairs.

His father was enraged! He tried to threaten, coax and cajole his son to change his ways and live a 'normal' life. But how can a God-intoxicated man ever return to worldly pursuits? Francis, to avert his father's wrath, hid himself in a cave near St. Damian's for a whole month. When he emerged from this place, emaciated with hunger and squalid with dirt, Francis was followed by a hooting rabble, who pelted him with mud and stones, and mocked him as a madman. Finally, he was dragged home by his father, beaten, bound, and locked in a dark closet. The father, who had been quite willing to indulge his son with enough pocket money for his pleasure pursuits, now felt that he could not continue to support him for his spiritual pursuits. Francis was told that he could no longer look to his family for support, if he persisted in his service activities. The decision was easy for Francis: he renounced his heritage and his life of wealth; it is said that he even gave up the clothes he wore, which were a symbol of his patrimony.

About this time, Francis happened to hear a sermon that transformed his life utterly and completely. Based on Jesus's injunctions to His Apostles, it stirred Francis to such an extent, that he would begin his life anew, with the words of Jesus, quoted in Matthew, 10 – 4.:

"Heal the sick, raise the dead, cleanse the lepers, cast out demons. Freely you received, freely give. Do not acquire gold or silver or copper for your money belts, or even a bag for your journey, or even two coats, or sandals, or a staff; for the worker is worthy of his support."

Francis resolved, then and there, to embrace the vow of poverty. He began to live as a beggar, as a wandering, homeless ascetic on the very streets that he had roamed as a carefree young man. Clad in a coarse garment, walking barefoot, and according to the Biblical precept, without staff or scrip, he began to preach the word of God.

Soon, like-minded souls joined Francis in his noble mission. Francis chose not to ordain them as priests, or even initiate a new order. He simply called his band of devoted souls, *fratres minores*, which, in Latin, means 'lesser brother'.

Thus it was that a pleasure-loving young man ceased his wanderings, voluntarily embraced poverty and returned to God.

The message of every *satsang* is 'go within'. Go Within. Explore your interior world and you will find that Divine Light which dispels every darkness.

Happiness, Where is Thy Abode?

India has given birth to many saints and sages. There are many true devotees of the Lord who have reached lofty spiritual heights. They have become *jeevan muktas* – liberated souls still in physical form on earth. But not all of them have become well known, or have been written about and recognised. To quote Gurudev Sadhu Vaswani's beautiful words, they have "lived a hidden life in the Hidden God." In terms of spiritual evolution, they have attained the purpose of this human birth: but alas, the people of this country know not even of their very existence!

Many of these great souls chose to live in seclusion: some of them chose caves and wooded areas in the Himalayas; some of them chose to live in the vicinity of holy rivers like the Ganga, Kaveri and Alaknanda; some of them chose the sacred city of Kashi as their home. Such was their spiritual *shakti*, that some people came to know about them and were drawn to them even in the anonymous condition they had chosen as their way of life. They acquired devout disciples who narrated the life stories of these saints to future generations. Some of them left great works of in literature and *kritis* (compositions) which were faithfully recorded by these devout disciples.

Today, I would like to tell you about one such saint: he lived in South India, in a quiet forest area far from the clamour of commerce and the haunts of men and the noise and crowds of critics. A few people came to know of his spiritual powers and were drawn to him. One such person, who was rich and affluent, took the saint's permission to build an humble *kutiya* in the forest for him. Inside the hut, was a marble platform, for the saint was known to spend days together in meditation, often dwelling in a state of *samadhi*. There was a courtyard around the hut; it was secured by a padlocked gate. The gate was always kept locked.

This might set some of you wondering: Why does a saint, a realised soul, need to live in a locked dwelling? What are his worldly goods that he should need such protection from the people outside? And is it not wrong to try to confine a saint to any single dwelling by restricting his free movement?

Let me say to you, I have heard of many holy men and saints, who dwelt in such locked premises, not to keep themselves away from people, but because the people who knew them and loved them, wished to assure these saints of their privacy and safety. It is said that the great saint known as Bhabaji who lived in the Himalayas, brought such grace and blessing to the people wherever he went, that in one village, the people decided to retain him in their midst permanently. They spoke to the forest guard whose cottage was situated just outside the village at the entrance to a forest. The guard was a pious soul who readily agreed to give up his 'quarters' allotted by the British government of those days. The saint was taken to the cottage; the guard secured a big lock and firmly secured the gate of the cottage;

the key was kept in his custody. Every day, the villagers brought their humble offerings of fruit and milk for the saint; the guard would open the gate and allow them inside; only a few people were allowed to enter at any given time. They would clean and sweep the cottage. At times, the saint was in a conscious state, spoke to them lovingly and gave them his blessings or even gave them his *upadesh*; at other times, he was in the super-conscious state of *samadhi*. On such occasions, the villagers, under the watchful eye of the guard, took great care not to disturb him. Fruits and milk were left for him, freshly bought day after day; sometime, these offerings were left untouched; the villagers took them away as *prasad*, leaving fresh offerings everyday without fail.

Saints do not need locks and keys; they do not need to guard their worldly possessions; in fact, in those days, many of them had none! They walked the little way and they were not famous; only a few people knew their power and grace, and even they were so respectful that they did not trouble the saints in any way.

You will understand now, the reason for the padlocked gate outside the saint's *kutiya*. And the saint I speak of was an *avadhuta*; one who did not cover his body with clothes. He had adopted *maun vrat* – the vow of silence for life. Little wonder then, that his devout disciples wished to offer him an undisturbed environment. And so it was that an affluent man had constructed this *kutiya* in the forest and secured it with a padlocked gate, which was carefully guarded by the saint's disciples.

Just as in the Himalayan Bhaba's case, villagers took milk and fruits as their offerings to the saint; just as it happened with Bhaba, the food would sometimes be taken back, untouched; but the villagers knew and respected the ways of the saint. When he was in his normal state, they would flock to him for *darshan*; his loving looks and his beautiful smile and his hand raised in blessing were more eloquent than mere words! If they had any queries or problems, they would approach him and talk to him; he often answered them in writing, using a pencil and a piece of paper which his assistant always had in readiness for him.

It was with good reason that the gate to the *kutiya* was padlocked. In the days gone by, the saint had lived in a small shelter, open on all sides. It is said that one day, the saint was sitting in *samadhi*. He sat with eyes wide open, but he was actually seeing with the eyes of his inner consciousness; in other words, he was lost to the world!

There is a passage from the *Aitareya Upanishad* which raises the question: Who is this Self, whom we desire to worship? Is he the self by which we see, hear, etc.? Is he the heart and mind by which we perceive? No, says the Upanishad. These are but adjuncts of the Self. The Self itself is Pure Consciousness. He is what we call Brahman. He is God, He is Brahma, He is Vishnu, He is Shiva, He is all Gods; He is also the five elements – earth, air, space, water, fire; He is all beings, great or small; He is all creatures that breathe the breath of life; fish, insects, birds. The reality behind all these is *Brahman*, who is pure Consciousness. Consciousness is *Brahman*.

This was the Absolute Reality with which the saint was in touch; the apparent reality, the illusory reality of the manifest world was lost on him! His senses were totally withdrawn; he was inwardly focussed on the Divine.

Many hours passed by. The saint sat in his state of *samadhi*, when a drunkard walked in. Seeing a man with his eyes open, the drunkard went inside and sat in front of the saint. Feeling magnetically drawn to the saint, the drunkard began to talk to the saint. But he received no answer. Angered by the silence of the saint he began to scream. As we all know, a drunkard can be quite unpredictable. He can even become violent and aggressive. So it happened with this drunkard. Unable to elicit any response from the saint for all his incoherent ramblings, he began to scream loudly. Still finding the saint unresponsive, he actually began to beat the saint and pull his beard. The villagers heard his screams and rushed to the spot. Aghast by his presence near their beloved saint, they dragged him away before he could do any further harm to the holy man. In their anger and rage, they would probably have beaten the offender to death; but the saint came to consciousness and signaled to them to stop beating the drunkard. He urged them to let him off and they obeyed him.

Later, when they gathered around the saint, he wrote a message for them: "You must not harm anyone; if you had killed that man, I would have felt that you had killed me!"

The people were absolutely devoted to the saint. They obeyed him implicitly. But now they were afraid for his safety; so it was that the rich devotee built a *kutiya* for him and the villagers insisted that the gate was secured with a padlock. The key was entrusted to the assistant, who dwelt just outside, ever ready to attend to the saint.

There was a seeker in spiritual quest, who came to know of the saint and sought to have his *darshan*. He asked his friend, who was also spiritually inclined, to accompany him in his journey to the saint's abode. With painstaking efforts, they managed to locate the village where he lived, and took directions to reach his *kutiya* in the forest. They were surprised to find the gate bolted and locked. They walked all around the hut, and found no way to get in. The windows of the hut were open, and they saw the saint sitting in a lotus posture, his eyes open and fixed on the far-away. Excited to have seen him at last, they called out to him: "Swamiji, we have heard so much about you! Please permit us to come in and touch your feet!"

But they received no reply from the saint. They saw that his eyes were open. They rattled the lock, banged on the door and called out loudly, "We have come to have your *darshan*. Please let us in!"

The assistant who had gone to fetch water from a nearby river, returned at this point. He was alarmed to see the newcomers knocking and banging at the gate, even though they appeared to be good, peaceful men. He gently persuaded them to come away from the gate and took them aside.

"Please open the door for us to have *darshan* of the saint," they pleaded with the *sevak*. The *sevak* replied, "I cannot open the gate for you just now. The Master is in a state of *samadhi*. He observes permanent silence. We do not permit anyone to disturb him at such times. I suggest that you wait for a while. When he permits us to have his *darshan*, I will take you to him, with his prior permission."

Realising their mistake, the seekers were truly contrite, and decided to wait patiently outside the gate. For hours, they waited; the saint was in deep *samadhi* and was unaware of their presence.

The *sevak* realised that they were genuine seekers. He also knew that sometimes, the saint would remain in his state of *samadhi* for days together. So he relented and allowed the men to enter the *kutiya* and just sit before the saint. He reasoned that even if they were unable to greet the saint and offer him their respects, they could at least reap the benefit of being in his holy presence, and absorbing the holy vibrations that emanated from him.

The men sat before the saint, their eyes and attention firmly fixed on his countenance. His eyes were open, and they actually saw tears trickle down from his eyes. For a long, long time these two friends sat opposite the saint, just looking at him. What they saw was unbelievable.

Tears fell from the eyes and the eye balls slowly moved up till the iris disappeared under the eyelids. The eyeballs rolled back to their original position leaving the eyes shivering. The body of the saint shook visibly. He took a deep breath and it appeared that he was gradually returning to his normal consciousness.

Seeing the two men seated in front of him, the saint smiled. He wrote on a piece of paper, "You have waited for me for a long time! If you wish to ask me a question, I will try to answer it as best as I can."

The first seeker said to the saint: "Swamiji, you dwell on this earth plane with the rest of us. But you seem to have risen above body consciousness. Your eyes were open, and yet they did not see anything. You do not seem to feel the cold or the heat. How did you get to this high level of spirituality?"

The saint smiled and wrote on the paper, "The body is gross and physical, you can train it as you like. You can control it. The physical body will always obey your commands. It can be regimented as per your requirement. Control over the body is no sign of spirituality. What you see is just the physical, and not a manifestation of the inner *atmic shakti.*"

The two men begged him, "Please guide us. There are many problems in this world which are beyond our ability to solve. But they impede our progress on the spiritual path. How can we handle them and keep our quest alive?"

In reply, the saint wrote, "You want to understand the world and solve its problems; but you will not be able to understand them, until you first understand who you are. First and foremost, know yourself. When you have attained self knowledge, you may try to understand the world and its problems. Know thyself. You have come here in quest of the truth, but the truth lies within you. Do not look for answers outside. Seek within, for within you lies hidden the invaluable treasure of knowledge. Go within."

"Go within!" These are words that each one of us must treasure. They show us the way to the truth, they represent true wisdom. We are so taken up with the world outside, that we live in utter ignorance of the spiritual treasures within us! We need to go within and discover the Absolute Reality.

The two friends placed yet another question before the saint. "How may we go within?"

The saint replied in writing, "The starting point of the inner journey is simplicity itself. Every day at a fixed hour sit in silence and look deep within."

"But Swamiji, we have tried this. As we sit in silence and go within we see darkness and the mind begins to wander."

The saint replied, "True. Very true. You see darkness because you are still under the control of your senses. You have created the darkness for yourself. If you want to be away from darkness then control your thoughts and you will move out of darkness into light."

The two friends asked, "Swamiji, can we experience *samadhi*?"

The saint replied to them, "Why not? All of us can experience divinity, but we need determination. I invite you to stay with me for some days, so that you too will experience the bliss of *samadhi*."

There are many more interesting stories of this saint, but the one we have discussed today carries a message for all of us. Go within. Know yourself. Go deep within. Control your thoughts and direct them away from the outer world to the inner world. Meditate in silence and be ever blessed!

Spend some time in silence, every day! Put to yourself the question, again and again — What am I? Whence have I come? Where is my true Homeland? Why am I here? One day, the answer will come to you out of the depths within. And to you will be revealed the Secret of Life. You will see, and you will know!

What Am I?

What is the purpose of this human birth?

The answer to this question is beautifully given by Gurudev Sadhu Vaswani in one of his books. He writes, "The main purpose of our life is to know our True-Self. The Goal of life is to realise the Self."

Gurudev Sadhu Vaswani urges us to dive within, to gather the pearls from the ocean of life. While we are here upon this earth, we should earn something which is everlasting, precious and priceless. For life is a school, a place of learning. We experience many things here, both pleasant and unpleasant. Every experience teaches us a lesson. And one of the most important lessons that we must learn is to appreciate the value of this human birth!

In His infinite kindness, God has given us the human birth as a gift. The human birth is an opportunity to fix and achieve our true goal. The physical body is but an instrument, a vehicle through which the eternal can be realised. In this world there are billions of species in which life exists in different forms but it is only the human species that has the intelligence to transcend the illusionary world and attain the higher self. Our intelligence has taken us to the moon and the stars. This intelligence has been given to us so that we may realise our Higher Self.

If you have read the Life of Sri Krishna, you will come to know that the many demons whom He killed in his early days at Brindaban, all attained salvation at His hands. Kaliya, the poisonous many-hooded serpent who took shelter in a lake in the Yamuna River near Brindaban, was one such demon. He was so poisonous, we are told, that the entire stretch of water which he inhabited was turned to poison, all trees on the bank withered away except for one, and even birds flying over that area would die from the poisonous fumes emanating from the lake...

Krishna went to the lake to get the great poisonous serpent out of the Yamuna. He stood on the one tree which was not dead [a *kadamba* tree] and jumped into the Yamuna. A fierce fight ensued between Kaliya and Krishna.

When the *gopas* and *gopis* heard about it, they crowded on the banks of the lake to watch the fight; they were fearful for their beloved Krishna, for they did not realise that He was the Supreme Lord. They thought of Him as their beloved friend and fellow cowherd. The fight went on for some time, and as the enormous snake began to grow tired, Krishna started dancing on its hood, to the great delight of all the assembled cowherds. When Krishna was about to kill the demon, Kaliya's wives intervened and fell at Krishna's feet and pleaded for mercy. "You have danced on the hood of Kaliya," they said to him. "By placing Your holy feet on his head, You have freed him of all sin and impurity and granted him the status that very few devotees of the Lord can ever hope to attain. Indeed, the very purpose of his life has been fulfilled. He is the most fortunate of beings, for on his head are imprinted your Divine footprints. Free him from the evil of *maya* and grant him salvation."

And so it came to pass that the poisonous snake was not killed by Krishna. He was merely asked to leave the vicinity of the Yamuna River and asked to go and live elsewhere. Thus Kaliya achieved liberation; the purpose of his life was fulfilled by the Lord's infinite grace.

If such is the Lord's grace for evil demons - consider how he would look upon us, His humble devotees!

It is sad that in spite of being bestowed with this precious gift of human birth, we have wasted it in making money, seeking pleasures, acquiring arts and skills which have value only on the earth plane. We forget to acquire the most important skill, the skill that will make us realise that we are immortal souls. We are so caught up in pursuing worldly affairs that we forget the main purpose for which we are on this earth. Our purpose here is not to eat, drink and make money; it is to know that we are not the bodies we wear, but the immortal souls that dwell within.

Let us always remember: I am not this physical body; I am not even the mind!

When I urge you not to identify yourself with the body, I am asking you to move away from the allures of the materialistic world. The more we identify ourselves with the body, the more we want, the more we crave, the more we possess, the more we get entangled in *maya*.

Once upon a time, there lived a wise and holy sage who had attained spiritual illumination. Many were the people who knocked at his door, eager to see him, speak to him and be blessed by him.

Whenever there was a knock at his door, he would ask "Who are you?" The visitor would invariably say, "I am so-and-so, son of so-and-so, from such-and-such-village."

"Why have you come?" the sage would ask next.

"O holy one, give me your blessings so that..." and the visitors would place their desires before the holy one. "So that I can have a rich harvest...", "So that I may have a son..." and so on.

Receiving such answers, the sage would lapse into silence. He would not open the door. Thus many people came to him and went away disappointed.

One day, a seeker came to knock at the holy man's door.

"Who are you?" called out the sage.

"I wish I knew," came the answer. "Oh holy one, I beg you to enlighten me, for I don't know who I am, and why I came into this world. Please show me the way, so that I may attain the true goal of this, my human life."

The holy man was well pleased with this reply and opened his door to admit the seeker. He realised that the man was a genuine aspirant, thirsting for the Truth. He took him as his disciple, and initiated him on the path of self-realisation.

Ask yourself, "Who am I?" Look for the answer in the heart within. "Where do I come from? Why am I here? What is the purpose of this existence of mine?" You will be led to the truth that you are not the body you wear!

Identification with the body leads to the illusion that power, pleasures and possessions of this world can make us happy. But this is not true; instead, these material possessions only keep us in bondage – the bondage of ignorance, *avidya*. Once you are freed from this illusion, you will realise the truth of the Self and move towards God-realisation. This is the process by which we may all move from illusion to reality; from darkness to light; from death to immortality.

A few days ago, there was a death in a family known to me. I visited them to offer my condolences. I found the dead man's widow crying loudly. She was calling out to him and pleading, "Dear one, why don't you answer me?" How could he answer? He was dead! How could he answer when he was not there, when he had left the physical body? The physical body was later taken to the cremation ground and was burnt to ashes.

The physical body had merged with the elements of nature but the soul had remained and made its transition to the other world. We are not the physical body nor the mind; we are the soul, which is a spark of the Divine, which is eternal and ever imminent! We are a permanent part of the Universe!

Do not remain under the illusion that you are a body-mind complex. You are much more than that. You are of the spirit. It is this, which you have to realise. To understand this you do not need explanation... You do not need reasoning. You need experience! This is an experiential process. You do not have to say - I am That, but you have to work to experience the truth - I am not this... I am That!

This does not mean that you have to neglect your body. I have said earlier, the physical body is the vehicle of the soul. It is like a horse you ride to reach your goal. A horse rider does not identify himself with the horse. But he takes immense care to look after the horse because the horse will take him to his destination. In the same way, we have to take care of this physical body because it is through this physical body that we shall reach our goal of self-realisation. But we must not identify ourselves with the bodies we wear.

Fortunate is the one who realise that this physical body is a vehicle to be used for the higher purpose of life. It is to be maintained and disciplined like a 'race-horse'.

If you get attached to the racehorse, and spend all your time in grooming it, forgetting to train it for the purpose for which it is bought, that is, to run a race and win the race for you, then you are sure to lose the race.

But this is what we normally do with our body. We groom it to the extent of forgetting that it is only a vehicle, that it is not an object to be beautified and worshiped for itself.

There are women who spend millions on their cosmetics, their dresses, their jewellery, their grooming and on their external appearances. They take immense care of their body from head to toe, polishing the exterior skin, nails, pampering their body with expensive lotions and perfumes. They forget that the real glow comes from within and for that, meditation, kindness and love are required. No amount of cosmetics can give you true beauty, which is the reflection of the inner soul...

Unfortunately, we think that we are this body and hence waste our time in grooming it. Instead we should work on our 'inner self' to achieve our goal of self-realisation.

The physical body is perishable, it is temporary; it is like the horse which has been hired for a limited period of time.

Similarly, our bodies are also temporary on this earth. One does not know when the body would give way, and when the messengers of death will come to call on us.

We are on a temporary lease on this planet earth; once the lease is over we have to go.

Sometime ago, a friend came to see me, accompanied by his son who had just acquired his first job in New Delhi. As luck would have it, the company had sent him to Pune on an official assignment. He had to travel to a suburb of Pune to visit one of the suppliers to his company. Travelling on official duty, he was allowed expenses, and had hired a taxi for a whole day. But his work at the supplier's office was over very quickly. So he brought the taxi home and invited his parents to use the taxi as they wished for the rest of the afternoon. My friend decided to come over to the Mission to meet me. I invited the family to stay over for lunch, but my friend declined the offer politely. "We have three hours time left with the taxi, Dada," he explained. "We want to make full use of the time and the mileage already paid for."

When we hire a car or a house, we have to pay its rent. If we have made good use of the car or of the house then we feel it's worth it, but, if we have not utilised the car or the house fully and yet paid the rent, then we feel it is a total loss.

In the same way, if we do not make proper use of the vehicle - called the physical body, then we have wasted the precious gift of the human birth.

When I was young, I loved riding a bicycle. I did not own one, so I would hire it. One day I hired a bicycle and parked it in the mission compound. I was very busy that day, and could not go out on the bicycle as I had planned. At the end of the day when I went to return it I told the owner that I had not used the cycle during the day. The owner said to me it was immaterial whether I had used it or not; I had hired it for the day so I had to make the payment for the whole day.

Whether we use this vehicle for the purpose for which we have received it or not, we still have to pay its price.

As I said earlier, you are not the physical body or even the mind. You are the light within. Hence, do not identify yourself with the body; it will only drag you into the pit of desires from where it is difficult to come out, and the cycle of birth and death will continue.

Take this message with you today. The goal of life is: "Know thyself"!

Time is running out on all of us. Death does not come with a prior announcement. Life is uncertain. Hence, begin your search for the truth now and here. You have to begin your quest by understanding the difference between the 'Lower Self' and the 'Higher Self'.

We have to overcome the physical and the mental; we have to overcome the emotional and the rational to be able, by God's grace, to see the beauty of the inner light!

Have you ever come upon a field full of flowers? Have you got up to watch the glorious sunrise that happens morning after morning? Have you felt the gentle breeze brush your face and ruffle your hair? Have you inhaled the scented night air and looked at the moon and stars with awe and wonder?

Wherever There is Beauty, There is GOD

When we are not rushing around attending to our worldly tasks, when we are not stressed with our workload, when we are not preoccupied with our thousand cares and anxieties – in short, when we actually allow ourselves to pause and just look all around us, we become aware of the beauty and magnificence of the world that God has created for us.

For many of us, this is an awareness that does not come easily or naturally. I do not mean the 'special' sights we see when we are abroad, or taking a vacation at a scenic spot. Nor do I refer to the feverish haste with which we 'click' pictures on our cellphones and digital cameras.

I mean the true awareness of the everyday world that we see from the windows of our home and office; the sky, the sunshine, the moonlight and stars, the trees, the greenery all around us, the birds, the squirrels, the grass underfoot, the flowers and the sparrows that come to perch on our window sills – are we taking note of the silent, ever present panorama of nature that unfolds daily before us? And when we actually experience this awareness at one of those precious moments when the beauty of the created world takes our breath away, do we stop to admire the handiwork of the great Creator?

And the beauty of God's creation is not limited to the world of nature: the radiant innocence of children, the beauty, grace and charm of women and the laughter and courtesy of men...God's hand is visible in them all!

What a wonderful thing it is – that the Lord is to be seen and felt in every aspect of his magnificent creation! We perceive the beauty of the created universe every moment that our eyes are open – but alas, we do not behold Him, for our eyes are veiled by *avidya* – ignorance. We fail to realise that He is with us, He is in all that we see, that He is watching us, watching over us all the time!

A young man was walking along the road, when all of a sudden, his eyes fell on a thousand rupee note lying on the ground. He could not believe what he saw – he could not believe that he was so lucky! Quickly he pocketed the currency note, making sure that nobody saw him. "How fortunate I am," he thought, "I have struck gold!"

From that day onward, his eyes were glued to the ground, whenever he went out walking. He failed to perceive the blue skies, the greenery all around, the distant hills and the colorful crowds that passed him by – his obsessive concern was all about the odd currency note that he might find once again, if he were so lucky!

We are all no different from this young man. We derive a little pleasure, enjoy some comforts in our worldly life – and all our attention and efforts are focused on these worldly pleasures. We lose ourselves to such an extent in our worldly existence, that we become blind to everything else around us.

The Upanishads tells us: *Isha Vasyam Idam Sarvam*. All that is, is a vesture of the Lord. The rivers, the hills, the woods, trees, plants, flowers and grass, the blue skies, the sun, the moon and the stars, the people, the places – all that you see around you, is the vesture of the Lord. Lift the veil, and you will behold God in everything you see. God watches you every moment, wherever you turn.

Sometime ago, I met a lady who keeps travelling continuously, so fond is she of touring. I asked her, "Doesn't all that travel make you tired?" Her reply was beautiful. "How can I ever grow tired?" she shot back. "Wherever I go, whatever I see, I think upon the Lord. I behold the beauty of His creation and bow down in reverence. To me, the beauty and magnificence of this world is but the shadow of the Lord."

Some people do admire the beauty of nature but many of them fail to perceive the presence of the Lord in what they admire so much. If only we had the awareness to behold Him in all that we see, admire the miracle of His creation in the world around us and bow down to the divine presence everywhere, how blessed we should be!

Gurudev Sadhu Vaswani loved to spend time in the lap of nature. He would choose a beautiful spot – on the bank of a stream or a garden. He loved to sit under the shade of a tree. He would often say to us, "Nature has taught me valuable lessons. The closer I am to nature, the more I gain in inner purity." He was a saintly soul, who was blessed with innate purity of spirit. But he would draw our attention to the healing, soothing, elevating, inspiring power of Nature and say to us repeatedly: "The closer you are to nature, the more you will grow in purity and radiance and inner perfection. You will also learn the virtue of humility and serenity."

"There is no need for the true seeker to turn away from the world," he said to us again and again. "All that we see around us, reminds us of the Lord's presence. What are we running away from?"

I have come across many holy men who say that they will not touch money. My Beloved Master used to say, "If you wish to give me money, I will accept it gladly. But I will not keep it with me – I shall spend it all, in the service of the poor, the weak and the suffering ones." For he beheld the Lord in them all; he beheld the Lord in the poor and the lowly.

We have no need to turn our back upon the world. We can stay in the world – with the awareness that all that we see, all that we hear, all that happens to us testifies to the Lord's omnipresence, omniscience and omnipotence. When man attains this state of profound awareness, he no longer looks upon the created universe as *maya* or illusion. To him, all the world is God's *leela* – the play of His Divine Will. In his heart arises the fervent prayer

Jidhar dekhta hoon
udhar tu hi tu hai
Ke har shai mein jalwa tera ruhbarooh hai
Beloved, I see you wherever I turn!

God is all around us. His Divine Will is manifest in all that happens to us. In every incident, every accident of life, we can behold the meaning of God's mercy. But alas, we only look for what is good and what is bad for us; we fail to see His Hand in all that happens.

The man of awareness says to the Lord: "I see thee in every incident, in every accident, in every condition, in every circumstance of life! I see Thee in everything that is around me!

Jidhar dekhta hoon, udhar tu hi tu hai...

My Beloved Master once narrated to us an instance of his profound communion with God. In one of those radiant moments he enquired of the Lord, "Dear Lord, I pray thee tell me, to whom does the beauty of this universe belong? What is the origin, the source of this beauty?"

The Lord said to him in reply, "Nothing but My Self, My Presence permeates this beauty that you behold. All this beauty is of Me and reflects what I am."

Aashiq bi main hoon, mashooq bi main hoon ishq bi main hoon
For I am the Lover, the Beloved and Love itself....

There are two types of men. The first cannot look below the surface of life. Such a man only confronts the apparent and is taken in by the joys and sorrows that come to him. The second sees the hand of God in everything, every condition of life. Wherever he turns, he glimpses the Lord. The first man is always in the throes of *maya*, illusion. He is bound by his own passions and desires and cannot free himself from his own bonds. The second man is happy, for he remembers the Lord constantly, and sings His praise and beholds the Lord wherever he turns.

Many of us, when we behold a beauteous form, tend to get carried away by the external appearance alone. We lose sleep; we lose our peace of mind. In truth, the beauty we have seen is God's; but we fail to perceive the truth behind the appearance, and become the slaves of the outer form alone.

Mark Antony was one of the greatest Generals of the Roman empire, at a time when Rome was at the height of its power and glory. Many were the battles he had fought, and vast were the territories that Antony had conquered for Rome. When the Roman Tribunes set their sights on Egypt, it was Mark Antony who was chosen to lead the campaign against that country.

At that time, Egypt was ruled by Cleopatra. She was a beautiful woman. Her form and features were akin to an exquisite marble statue carved by a master sculptor. Cleopatra realised that her small army stood no chance against Antony's vast and powerful Roman legions. She would be vanquished, and her country simply overrun by the conquerors. She therefore decided that she would use her secret personal weapon to defeat Antony – her own beauty and charm. "I shall enslave the Roman General with my beauty," she decided. 'I shall win, despite the power of the Roman army."

With this determination did Cleopatra confront Antony; and the brave and valiant soldier, who was victor of many battles and the architect of great conquests, fell before her charms. His patriotism, his loyalty to Rome, his great reputation as a soldier and his duties as a general were all forgotten, as he became Cleopatra's willing slave. Every nerve of his body, every fibre of his being was obsessed by his passion for her.

The Roman Empire needed Antony's presence urgently. He had been sent to conquer Egypt, and now he lived a soft life in Egypt, vanquished by its Queen. The Romans sent him urgent and frantic messages: "Rome needs you. The magnificent River Tyber awaits your return." Antony's response was that of a man blinded by love.

"Burn Tyber! Let Rome in Tyber melt!"

All he wanted out of life was Cleopatra. She had become a barrier, an obstacle between the conqueror and the fulfillment of his destiny as a Roman. He died in ignominy, taking away his life with his own hands, shamed by defeat and humiliation.

In truth, Cleopatra's beauty was just a shadow of the Lord's radiance. But Antony was ensnared by her feminine charms, and could not see beyond external appearances. If only we could look beyond the veil, and recognise God's presence!

Charles Parnell was a great patriot, a true nationalist who led the Irish struggle for freedom. He was a magnificent and powerful orator, whose words seemed to cast a magic spell over his listeners. Profoundly inspired by his fervent nationalist discourses, women would remove all the gold and silver ornaments they wore, and donate it all to the cause of the Irish nationalist freedom.

At one of these nationalist gatherings, Parnell met Katherine O'Shea, a beautiful woman who had come to listen to him. She listened to him attentively from the front row. When Parnell's eyes fell on her, the direction of his life took an unexpected turn. So smitten was he by her charms, that he put everything behind her: everything that he had struggled for – Ireland, Home Rule for Ireland, the cause of Irish freedom – everything took second place after Katherine O'Shea. What was even more tragic, was the fact that she was a married woman, the wife of his own colleague in Parliament! He was cited as co-respondent in a divorce suit filed by her husband; he did not contest the case, because he wanted Katherine to be divorced, so that he could marry her.

He married her of course. But he was rejected by a majority of his party members, and deposed from his position as "the uncrowned king of Irish politics". The Church denounced him, for they felt that "by his public misconduct, he had utterly disqualified himself to be a leader." The common people also felt betrayed by the man in whom they had placed their trust. It was a spectacular ruin of a promising political career. Ireland too, paid a heavy price for his indiscretion. For the Irish Home Rule Bill was shelved by the British parliament.

Saints and holy men urge us to behold God's presence in all the beauty that we see around us. "When you perceive beauty in created forms, remember the Creator. How beautiful He must be, to have been the Architect of all the beauty we see!"

Sri Ramakrishna would often laugh at Englishmen, who loved to spend time in woods and gardens, exclaiming, "How beautiful! How beautiful!" He pointed out how these great admirers of nature, failed to look beyond the manifest beauty to the Unmanifest – the Divine Beauty and Power of the Creator.

Alas, we live in oblivion of the Creator, when all the beauty of nature around us fails to awaken our awareness of His presence. Therefore let all beauty serve to us as a reminder of the Lord, and His countless blessings upon us. We need constant reminders of His presence, even as we move along the pathways of life. The world of Nature and all of Humanity serves as a constant reminder, proclaiming His beauty and His Divine Presence to us. Blessed is the man who beholds the Lord in everything he sees, everyone he meets. But this is possible, only when our eyes and mind are pure and enlightened.

Sri Krishna tells Arjuna in the Bhagavad Gita: "Conquer your senses. Obtain total control of your senses. For these are like powerful, galloping horses. Harness them aright, and they will lead you to God. If you set them free, they will lead you on the wrong path!"

We may conquer our senses only through *sadhana* – constant practice. When we acquire *ekagrita* or one pointedness, we learn to meditate, and we come to realise that the Lord's presence is everywhere and He sees us constantly. All we have to do is learn to glimpse His presence in all that we see.

Jidhar dekhta hoon, udhar tu hi tu hai
Ke har shai mein jalwa tera ruhbarooh hai ....

Behind every experience—pleasant or unpleasant — is the Lord Himself. Unmask the experience and behold the Face of Reality. Therefore, accept everything. Accept, Rejoice! And move on!

Mantra For The Modern Man

One of the questions people ask me most often is: Do you think it is possible for anyone to lead a life of peace in these troubled times?

My reply is: It is not only possible; it is your birthright. Yes, *ananda*, bliss, the peace that passeth, nay, surpasseth understanding is your birthright! You are a child of God — and He is the source of eternal bliss, unending bliss. The moment you realise that you are a child of God, you will let nothing affect you. All you need to do is forget yourself — and realise your true self as a child of God. When we forget this outer self, transcend the phenomenal, material world, we draw closer to the real, inner self, which is peace.

What is peace? I may tell you what peace is in many words, but all descriptions will fail and you will not understand those words until you have felt peace in the heart within!

Like love, peace must be felt!

Perhaps many of us often ask ourselves, "Why is there no peace in our hearts?" God has blessed us abundantly; we live in comfortable homes; we eat good food; we have enough money to spend on necessities as well as a few luxuries. Why is it then that peace eludes us?

A few days ago, a sister from Mumbai came to meet me. She belonged to a well-known, well-to-do family. She requested for a private meeting with me; and when I met her, she began to shed tears. She said: "Dada, there is one thing that I can't come to terms with. I have money aplenty; there are servants to carry out my every bidding; we have several cars and bungalows; my children are very attached to me and pay attention to my every need and comfort. And yet – and yet, I know not why I am so unhappy! I feel so depressed that quite often, I shut myself alone in my room and weep bitterly! I cry out to God in grief and frustration, 'Lord, why is it thus with me?' For God has given me everything – except happiness. Why, Dada, why is this so?"

This is the condition of many of us. We have everything we need – and we are still unhappy. What is the reason of this pervasive unhappiness in the world?

Friends, the key to happiness is Peace of Mind. He who is blessed with peace of mind is always happy – even if he is penniless and he owns nothing in this world. Saints, great souls and renunciates have nothing to call their own; yet are they radiantly happy. Such was the *dervish* who said: "Nothing in the morn have I and nothing do I have at night. Yet there is none on earth happier than I!"

Lord Krishna tells Arjuna in the Bhagavad Gita: "Arjuna, *ashantasya kutah sukham*? If man is not at peace with himself, how can he be happy?" The key to happiness – indeed, the secret of true happiness is peace of mind.

We lack peace of mind, because our minds are restless; our minds wander constantly; and we wander with the mind. All day long, the mind wanders, dragging us along with itself; nor are we still and restful at night. Even in dreams does the mind wander; and we struggle ceaselessly in its wanderings. Therefore it happens that we are never at peace.

How then can we stop the mind from wandering? Arjun asks of Sri Krishna. "O Lord, Thou hast said that the wandering of the mind is the cause of all human sorrow. Pray tell me then, how can we stop the mind from wandering?"

Lord Krishna tells him: "It is difficult, but not impossible to control the mind." Indeed, it is possible for each one of us to conquer the mind and bring it fully under control. For this, two things are necessary: *vairagya* and *abhyasa*. It is only with a guru's grace that we can attain these two qualities. As we cultivate reverence for the guru, the impulse arises within us to follow the path of *abhyasa* or practice of spiritual discipline. Many people make this effort, but only those blessed with the guru's grace succeed in their efforts. Such blessed souls follow the path of *abhyasa* successfully, and gradually attain to the state of *vairagya* or detachment. It then becomes possible for them to control the mind, and inner peace soon follows. He who is blessed with inner peace is happy in every state, every condition of life.

To take you back from the effect to the cause: Why is it that we lose our peace of mind? Because our wishes, our desires are crossed. We want a particular thing to be done in a particular manner. When it happens in a different way, perhaps in exactly the opposite way, our peace is lost.

There is one way of achieving peace of mind. That is to attain the realisation that all that happens, happens according to the will of God.

Gurudev Sadhu Vaswani used to tell us, "God upsets our plans to set up His own. And His plans are always perfect."

If I have the faith that whatever has happened to me is according to the plan of the Highest, that there is some hidden good in it for me, I will not be upset! Gurudev Sadhu Vaswani also used to say, "Every disappointment is His appointment. And He knows best."

Once you realise this, there is no more frustration, no more unhappiness. You abide in a state of tranquility and peace. You may not be able to achieve this straight away. It is a process through which you must move.

May I pass on to you a *mantra* which is sure to bring you peace? It is a prayer which a saint, a holy man of God used to offer again and again. Inscribe it on the tablet of your heart. Repeat it again and again — remember it by day and night, for it is really simple:

Yes Father, Yes Father — Yes and always yes!

Yes Father, Yes Father — Yes and always yes!

There are people who are upset with me because I advocate the philosophy of acceptance. They say to me, that this will make people lazy and lethargic; they will give up all their drive and ambition and simply sink into passive resignation.

I beg to differ! People who believe in the supremacy of the Almighty, people who learn to accept His Divine Will, never ever give in to lethargy and pessimism. They do as the Lord bids them in the Gita — they put in their best efforts; they do not slacken; they do their best to achieve what they want. But if they do not achieve the desired results, they do not give in to despair and frustration; they do not give in to disappointment.

An inspector of schools visited our St. Mira's School in Pune. During an interaction with the students, he asked them, "Tell me, where is Pune situated?" Many hands shot up, and the children gave the answer in chorus, "In the State of Maharashtra."

"Where is Maharashtra?" the inspector persisted.

"In India," said the children.

"And where is India?"

"In Asia."

"Can you tell me where is Asia?"

"In the world."

"And where is the world?"

A pregnant silence prevailed. But one little girl came out with a sterling answer. "Sir, the world is safe in the hands of God!"

The world is safe in the hands of God! Why then should we lose our sleep and peace of mind?

There are so many situations and circumstances in life that shatter our peace. But how long can we allow ourselves to wallow in sorrow and self-pity? The call of life is Onward, Forward, Godward! Men may come and men may go, but life goes on forever! Lives may come to an end, but life on earth must go on!

"Would you know who is the greatest saint in the world?" asks William Law. "It is not he who prays most or fasts most; it is not he who gives most alms or is most eminent for temperance, charity or justice; but it is he who is always thankful to God; who wills everything God wills, who receives everything as an instance of God's goodness and has a heart always ready to praise God for it."

It is said that the Pilgrim Fathers — the early European settlers in America — "made seven times more graves than huts." That is, hundreds of them lost their lives, only a handful survived, but at the cost of losing their near and dear ones. Thus their settlements had "more graves than huts". And yet, they set aside a special day for Thanksgiving! They knew what it is to accept the will of God!

Yes Father — Yes and always Yes!

Acceptance in the spirit of gratitude unlocks the fullness in our lives. It can turn despair into faith, strife into harmony, chaos into order, and confusion into clear understanding. It restores peace into our hearts and helps us to look forward to the morrow in the faith that God is always with us!

It is not enough to speak of gratitude or enact deeds of gratitude — we must live gratitude by practising acceptance of God's will in all conditions, in all incidents and accidents of life.

When things are not going as we wish, we tend to develop 'tunnel vision' — that is, focus on the dark, negative side of life. However, we will do well to remember that it is always darkest before dawn and trial and adversity can be powerful agents of change that help us grow, evolve to become better human beings, and eventually make a success of our lives.

There are several things in our lives about which we are not happy. Our 'wish list' for something different, something more, something other than what we possess extends to several aspects of our daily life.

Many affluent teenagers now carry cell phones — something unheard of even ten years ago. But not all of them are happy with these gadgets. Every six months or so, they wish to change models; they want more 'features'; they want the latest. When they are denied what they want, they sulk, they grumble, they wish they had richer and kinder parents.

Homemakers, mothers and wives wish to have better equipped kitchens; they want more gadgets, more equipment, more aids to make their life easy. They want better furniture, more expensive curtains, and nicer clothes to wear. Men want better jobs, a better boss, a bigger car, more money and more leisure.

There's nothing wrong in wishing for any of these things. The problem arises when we develop a feeling of active discontent with what we are and what we have. Discontent leads to depression, and depression destroys our peace of mind.

A psychiatrist has described depression as "anger turned inward". We are angry with so many things and so many people; we are discontented with the way we live our lives — and we are angry with ourselves.

It was St. Francis who prayed, "Lord give me the strength to change the things I can change, patience to accept the things I cannot change, and wisdom to know the difference."

Wisdom consists in accepting what you cannot change. What cannot be cured must be endured. This is not passive resignation or pessimistic self-denial. It is the way of wisdom which leads to peace.

We need to grow in the spirit of acceptance, for life is full of unexpected events. A dear one is snatched away from us suddenly. Initially, we are devastated; we weep, we shed bitter tears; we refuse to eat, we cannot sleep.

That is but natural, you might say. But how long can you go on? Will weeping, fasting and vigil bring your loved one back to life?

And then again, aren't we all mortal? Can we determine the length and duration of our own life — or anyone else's life?

Wisdom consists in accepting God's will — not with despair or resignation, but in peace and faith, knowing that our journey through life has been perfectly planned by Infinite love and Infinite wisdom. There can be no mistake in God's plan for us!

Again and again, we try to run away from difficult situations; again and again we rebel, react with anger and bitterness. How can we ever be at peace?

The answer is simple: grow in the spirit of surrender to God; develop the spirit of acceptance. "Not my will, but Thy will be done, O Lord!" this must be the constant utterance on your lips.

To seek refuge is to trust the Lord — fully, completely, entirely. It is to know that He is the one Light that we need in the darkest hours of our life. He is the all-loving One whose ears are ever attentive to the prayers of His wayward children. He is the all-knowing One who does the very best for us. With Him, all things are possible and if He chooses not to do certain things for us which we want Him to do, it is not because He cannot do them, but because He knows better — He knows we require something else for our own good.

So it is that he who has taken refuge in the Lord is ever at peace. "Not my will, but Thy will be done, O Lord," he prays. Whatever happens, "I accept! I accept! I accept!" is his *mantra*. "Yes Father, Yes and always Yes!" is his response to all incidents and all accidents of life. Nothing — no accident, no loss, no tragedy — can disturb his equanimity. Such a man is truly blessed. He has attained peace within.

Everything – and that includes everyone – we have really belongs to God. It is ours so long as He chooses to keep it with us. If He takes back anything, who can blame Him?

No One Belongs to Us

Saints, seers and sages remind us constantly: "O Man, never ever forget this truth: alone you came into this earth. Alone you shall depart from this earth. Nothing, no one on this earth, can you consider as your own."

Ko Kahu Ko Nahi
Ko Kahu Ko Nahi
Akela aaya, Akela rawana

Our thinking is different. We dwell on *our* own people – *my* father, *my* mother, *my* son, *my* daughter, *my* wife, *my* husband, *my* friend and so on. We will do anything for those whom we consider *our* own. We are prepared to help them at all costs; why, we are even ready to lie and cheat for them, and throw in a few wrong deeds too, if it is necessary to please them.

And yet the saints warn us:

Ko Kahu Ko Nahi
Ko Kahu Ko Nahi

Nothing and no one on this earth is yours.

There was a temple where *satsang* was being held regularly. The holy man who delivered the discourses emphasised this teaching repeatedly.

We came into this earth alone, alone shall we leave. No one shall go with us.

Ko Kahu Ko Nahi
Ko Kahu Ko Nahi

A devout man came to the temple everyday to hear the holy man's discourses. He thought to himself, "Surely, there is a lot of wisdom in what the *swamiji* tells us. But there is one thing that bothers me. Again and again, he tells us, *Ko Kahu Ko Nahi, Ko Kahu Ko Nahi.* Obviously, being a man of renunciation, the *swamiji* knows nothing of family ties and bonds! I, for instance, am not alone. Why, my beloved wife and my dear mother will do anything for me. How can I consider them as anything other than my own?"

When he could no longer keep his thoughts to himself, he decided to place them before the holy man. "*Guruji*," he said with reverence, "you tell us again and again that man is all alone in this world – that nobody can be called our own on this earth. I humbly submit to you that, I, sir, am definitely not alone. My wife and my mother are absolutely devoted to me. They will do anything for me – even lay down their own lives for me! They will never ever disown me! How then can I go around saying, *No one is mine*? They are my people. They are my very own!"

The saint smiled. It was not the first time that he had heard such doubts or objections from a member of his congregation.

"My dear son," he said to the man, "It is our great saints and seers who have taught us this profound truth – that nothing and no one on this earth is truly ours. Their words can never go wrong. If you like, you can put this truth to test, so that your doubts are cleared."

So saying, the holy man gave him a pill. "Take this pill when you go home and lie down," he said. 'Your eyes will close, your breath will seem to be still, and people will think you are dead. But you will be fully alert and conscious and you will be able to hear what is going on around you."

The man thought to himself, "The *swamiji* is undoubtedly wise. But there are a few things about this world that he will learn from my family today. My mother and my wife will prove to him that I am not alone – that they will lay down their lives for me!"

He went home and did exactly as the *swami* had instructed him to do. In a few minutes, his whole body grew cold and stiff, and he lay on his bed, perfectly still – to all appearance, dead.

Shortly afterwards, his wife came up to him. "Wake up, my dear!" she called. "It is time for dinner."

There was no reply from her husband.

Alarmed, she put her hand on his forehead, and found it cold. She shook him gently, he did not move. Trembling, she held her hand before his nostrils to feel his breath – and all was still!

In deep dismay, she called to her mother-in-law, "*Maaji*, do come here quickly and see what has become of your son!"

The mother came running to see what was amiss. She could not believe what she saw. Quickly, a doctor was summoned. He examined the man and pronounced him dead: "His pulse is down, and his heart has stopped beating," said the doctor. "He is no more with us."

The mother and wife were distraught. But they remembered the *swamiji* of whom the man had always spoken very highly. "There's still hope," they whispered to each other, as they sent word to the holy man, begging him to come to their house. Perhaps he would perform a miracle – and revive their loved one!

The holy man had been waiting for their call – for this whole play or *leela* had been scripted and produced by him! In no time, he was at the house of the devotee.

He saw the wife and mother weeping and wailing in profound grief. "O, what a terrible fate has befallen us!" they wept. "How can we live without our loved one? Why has God been so cruel to us? Why did He not take one of us instead? Of what use are our lives without him? What a terrible thing to happen!"

The man who lay as if he were dead, was aware of the *swamiji's* presence even as he heard his wife and mother cry in sorrow. "That should teach the *swamiji*," he thought to himself. "He will no longer tell me that there is no one to call my own in this whole wide world. He will surely change his mind now."

"Do not weep, ladies," the holy man said to them. "I can revive your loved one – on one condition."

The wife and mother were thrilled. "Whatever the condition, we will accept it," they said in unison. "Only, let him live again. We will do anything to have him alive and well with us."

"He will live," promised the saint, "provided one of you is prepared to give your breath to revive him. I mean, you must be prepared to end your own life, so that he may live. Is one of you prepared to die for him?"

The women were taken aback. The mother recovered, and was the first to speak up.

"I am old, and life holds no charms for me," she said. "Gladly will I offer my life to save my son. But alas, my responsibilities hold me back. I have two young daughters who are yet to be married. If I pass away, who will care for them? It is my duty to see them happily married, and I must obey the call of duty. Gladly will I die for my son – but I cannot choose to die before my duty to my daughters is complete."

"Not just this life, but a thousand lives shall I give up for the sake of my beloved husband," said the wife, casting a sharp glance at her mother-in-law. "But alas, my husband is still young. If I die to let him live, he will surely marry again; and a stepmother will take charge of my poor young children. Who knows how she will treat them? May be she will turn out to be harsh and cruel. How can I expose my beloved children to such a fate? I would willingly die for my husband – but I have to live for the sake of my children!"

The man heard all that was going on. He realised that the fact of the matter was that neither his wife, nor his mother were really ready to give up their life to save him.

"You can get up, now, my son," said the holy man. "You have heard everything, and you know that this place is not for you. Get up and follow me to seek the truth of life."

"I have learnt my lesson," said the man, as he got up to follow his guru. "No one on earth can I call my own. For each of us is alone, truly alone."

The *karmas* of our previous births determine that we are born into a particular family. We have certain duties, certain obligations to the members of our family, which we duly carry out. We love them; we make them feel that they are dearer to us than the whole world. But even as we do this, we must bear in mind: there is no one on earth that we can call our own. God alone is truly ours – and we are His alone. Our worldly relationships are all transient, ephemeral. There is only one lasting bond – our bond with God, who is the loving Father of us all.

Some of you may well ask me, "If we consider that we are all alone, and there is no one to call our own, how can we survive, how can we subsist in this lonely journey that is life?"

This question was put to Sri Ramakrishna Paramahansa by his disciples. "*Swamiji*," they said to him, "you tell us that each of us is alone, that we cannot call anyone our own. Tell us then, how we may live in this world, how we may move with the members of our family?"

Sri Ramakrishna narrated a beautiful parable in answer to their question. "Think of a maidservant – an *ayah* – who works in the house of a wealthy man. It is her job to care for his children. Her own family, her own children, live far away in her native village. She is working in the city to earn some money for her family. She cares for the Master's children lovingly; she bathes them, feeds them, plays with them and puts them to sleep. She carries the children in her arms, she gently swings them on her lap. But all the while, her thoughts are with her own children, far away in her native village. Conscientiously, she does her duty by the Master's children, but not for a moment does she regard them as her own. And never, ever does she forget her own children."

Sri Ramakrishna said to his disciples, "We must learn to live in this world, even as the *ayah* lives in her Master's home and carries out her duty."

We all have duties and responsibilities. We must carry them out as well as we can. But let us always carry the thought of our true home and of God with us. In the background of our consciousness, let us bear the thought that God alone is ours – and that, except for Him, we are all alone.

We live and move in our family circle. We eat with them; we sleep with them; we dwell in their constant presence. But still, we are on our own – God alone is ours, and we are His alone.

Ko Kahu Ko Nahi
Ko Kahu Ko Nahi
Akela, aaya, Akela rawana

What can we do to keep this awareness alive in our day to day life? There is one golden rule that we must follow – we must give first preference, first place to God in our lives, and to everything else, thereafter. If only we follow this golden precept, a beautiful transformation will be wrought in our lives.

Often, this is not what we do. We devote our time and effort to everything else – our work, our career, our family, our friends, our hobbies and pleasures and so on. If there is a little time left after all this, we grudgingly devote it to God. And we consider ourselves too busy, too burdened by responsibilities to think of God!

This is not as it should be. God should take priority in our lives. Our time and effort should be devoted to Him first and foremost – and what remains can be spent on our worldly responsibilities.

When a man is young, he concentrates his effort on pleasurable living; he wanders far and near, he enjoys life to the hilt. As he grows older, his thoughts turn to God. He feels the urge to seek God. He tries to meditate, focus his mind upon the Lord – but it is too late! The spirit is willing, but the flesh is weak. Old habits die hard, and he finds his mind and heart flooded with worldly thoughts, while he tries desperately to focus on God. If truth were to be told, he has never ever made the effort to achieve *ekagrita* – one-pointedness of the mind. Therefore, let us resolve here and now – to give God the first place in our lives. Nothing will affect us, nothing can harm us then.

If you add water to milk, the two will blend as one. But when butter is taken out of the milk, you will find that water does not mix with the butter. The butter floats on the surface of the water and the water stays separate from the butter. Thus should we make our life sublime. We should extract the butter of spirituality out of the milk that is worldly life. Then we will not be bound by the world anymore!

Look at a little child who holds fast on to a pillar, while he swings round and round. He is safe and secure as he swings around happy and cheerful. He is safe in the knowledge that he holds the pillar firmly; he cannot fall, for the pillar is his solid support; but if he lets go of the pillar, he will grow dizzy as he swings, and he will fall down.

God is the pillar of our existence. He is our strength and support. Let us cling to Him – and live our life through His grace. He is our unfailing Friend and Father; we need no one else except Him.

Ko Kahu Ko Nahi
Ko Kahu Ko Nahi
Akela, aaya, Akela rawana

The world is a bridge; we are all passers-by; we have to pass over this bridge; we cannot build our houses on this bridge; we cannot build, we cannot erect our buildings on this bridge; we have to move on.

The World is a Bridge

All thinking individuals find themselves reflecting on one particular question over and over again in the course of their lives: What is the meaning of this life that we lead? Where is it leading us? What is the purpose for which we have come here?

May I say to you, these questions have been placed before me by many brothers and sisters. Why are we here? What are we to make of this earthly life?

We are born into this world, and we grow up with so many hopes, aspirations, dreams and desires. And then, all of a sudden, we hear the call of Death; *Yama*, the Lord of Death, bids us depart from here without prior intimation, in many cases: "Dear brother / sister, it is time that you left." All our dreams, desires and hopes are left behind, as Man returns to the unseen realm where he came from. What then is the meaning of life? What is the nature of the world we live in?

Sometime ago, a lady came to meet me. She told me, "I was married 17 years ago. My husband loved me deeply – and I forgot everything else in the world except his love. My friends, my family, my relatives were all forgotten, so wrapped up was I in my marriage. Then, one fateful night, my husband passed away in his sleep. Alas, I have no idea what pain, what agony he must have gone through, as death claimed him. When I awoke, the next morning, and realised that my husband had gone away from me, never to return, I was crazy with grief. Ever since then, I have repeatedly asked myself – what is the meaning of human life?"

Many of us have passed through such experiences. We too, find ourselves perplexed by the same question – what does it all mean? What is life? What is this world which we call our home?

Saints and wise men have given us a variety of answers to these queries. One such response tells us: The world is a bridge. No one stops on a bridge. We simply have to cross the bridge and get to the other shore.

"The world is a bridge, pass over it, but build no houses upon it. He who hopes for a day, may hope for eternity; but the World endures but an hour. Spend it in prayer for the rest is unseen." Such is the inscription engraved on the *Bulund Darwaza*, the magnificent gateway to the deserted city of Fatehpur Sikri, built by Emperor Akbar. The saying is actually attributed to Jesus Christ, in the Islamic tradition.

In real life, we cross over bridges. On huge flyovers and expressway bridges we actually have warning signs telling us not to stop our vehicles, but to drive through. And yet we seek to build our dreams on the bridge that is earthly life!

There lived a Saint, who began his *padyatra* early every morning. He moved on from hamlet to hamlet, village to village, city to city, never stopping anywhere for long. Many of his disciples followed him, wherever he went. One day, as they went on their way, they came across a river in spate. There seemed to be no way of crossing the river – no boats or ferries were available. Far ahead, in the dim distance, they could see an old wooden bridge. They made their way to this bridge, and crossed the river. As they walked across the bridge, the Saint said to his disciples, "My dear ones, always remember, the world is very much like this bridge that we are crossing now. We cannot halt here; we must not stop, we have to keep moving onward, forward, till we get to the other shore."

"The world is a bridge," he repeated. "Pass over it, and build not thereon."

Of deep significance are these words. We must pass over the bridge of life – and not attempt to build on it. Of course, this does not mean that we stop building homes for ourselves. By all means, let us build homes; but let us not get attached to these homes and regard them as permanent. Our flats and bungalows and villas will have to be left behind us. For this world is a bridge – and we are birds from a distant land. We walk across the bridge for a short while, but our true home is afar – it is the land where shines the eternal lamp of the divine; the land where flows the *Ganga* of true knowledge, and the *Jamuna* of *Yoga*. Regrettably, having come to this earth, walking across the bridge that is life, we have forgotten our true identity. We have been enchained by the fetters of our desires. But go back we must – and we do not even know when the appointed hour of our return will come upon us.

I remember an incident that was narrated to me. There was a distinguished professor, who was the Principal of a reputed Engineering College. One day, he was approached by a group of final year students. Their representative said to him, "Sir, you know this is our final year in college. In a few days time, our class will break up for the exams. Our whole class would like to take a photograph with you, which we may keep as a souvenir."

The Principal readily agreed. A day was appointed for the class photograph; the college photographer was called, and he supervised the seating arrangements. Chairs, benches and tables were so arranged that all students could stand in rows, one behind the other. Everyone took their place, and the Principal took the chair placed in the center, amidst the group. The first shot was clicked.

"Please don't move," requested the photographer, readying the camera for another shot. As is customary with group photographs, he would click two shots, in case one should be lost. The students straightened themselves, and prepared for another pose.

"Smile please," said the photographer, as he surveyed the group through his lens. His eyes swept from one row to another to make sure everyone was in focus, when he realised with horror that the Principal had slumped to one side. His head was down, and his eyes were closed. Between the first shot and the second, even as he remained seated for the group photograph, death had come to claim him.

It is a life of impermanence that we lead here. It is a world of uncertainty in which we dwell.

Once, the disciples of Lord Buddha enquired of him, "*Gurudev*, please tell us what is human life."

Lord Buddha replied: "Thus shall you think of all this world. A star at dawn, a bubble floating on a stream, a flash of lightning on a summer cloud, a flickering lamp, a phantom and a dream."

What beautiful words. How beautifully they bring out the transience and impermanence of all life!

Guru Tegh Bahadur too, emphasises the same idea. "Life is nothing but a dream," he says. "How can we remain attached to that which will fade away in our sleep?"

If we would remember these two great truths – the first, that this world is but a bridge we must cross; the second, that we are birds from a distant land who have flown here – but have become enchained by our own desires, we would soon realise the true meaning of life.

We come to live upon this earth for a short while; but we begin to chase shadows and illusions; we become enslaved by our senses in pursuit of pleasures. Have you seen a fly hovering over honey? It is tempted by the honey, and wishes to taste it, just a little, and then fly away. Alas, that is just not possible. Having tasted the honey, the fly is trapped in the sticky sweetness; it struggles to escape, but in vain; and it meets its painful end in that sweet and cloying liquid, which becomes its death trap. The human condition is similar; enchained by our own passions and desires, we are trapped in the illusion that is life.

A man came to see me. Distraught, he said to me through tears, "Help me, help me! I have fallen victim to alcoholism. It all began as a new, a different kind of experience. My friends dared me and I only wanted to show them I was as bold and daring as they were; perhaps I wanted to find out what liquor tasted like. I thought to myself, I shall just take a small drink to see what it is like, but I found that I could not stop! I have become a slave to liquor now. My life and my business are in ruin. Can you please tell me how I may get out of the mess I am in? Can you please help me to kick this dreadful habit?"

Thus it is, that we come into this world and chase after shadow-shapes that lead us to destruction. One such shadow is money – wealth. Every one of us wants more and more money. And we are willing to do anything to get money, even commit fraud and sin.

How much money does a man need? One lakh? Ten lakhs? One crore? Alas, there is no limit to man's greed for wealth. He who has one million, wants to have one billion. As for the billionaire, he wished to become a multi-billionaire. Chasing after these shadow-shapes, man loses himself and his life. His lakhs, crores and millions are all left behind when he dies.

So it is that Guru Arjan Dev tells us in his *bani*, "He who is caught in the vicious cycle of desires, comes to naught."

There is an old English Morality play called *Everyman*. It opens with God commanding Death to go and summon Everyman to appear in Heaven before Him to face his final judgement. Death appears before Everyman and asks him to leave upon his final journey. Taken aback by the unexpected summons, Everyman calls upon all those whom he had valued and cherished in his life to accompany him on this dreaded journey: Fellowship, Kindred, Cousin and Goods (symbolically, these allegorical characters represent Friends, Family, Worldly Wealth). However, all of them refuse to accompany him. Fellowship tells him that he will be with him only for eating, drinking and making merry; Kindred and Cousin offer lame excuses; Goods, i.e. Material Goods tells him that his presence will only make the situation worse for Everyman. In utter fear, Everyman turns to Good Deeds, and requests her to accompany him. Good Deeds assures him that she will be with him; but Everyman has neglected her for the greater part of his life, and that has made her weak and frail; so she offers to bring her sister,

Knowledge, to guide them on the journey. Knowledge makes Everyman understand that he must repent for his sins and seek God's forgiveness. She also makes him realise that he will have to leave behind everything including herself, when he faces God for his final Judgement. Everyman's earthly qualities, Beauty, Strength, Discretion and Five Wits also desert him at the final moment; Knowledge stays with him till the final moment, but she too must be left behind. Good Deeds alone goes with him till he reaches Heaven.

The moral of the story is obvious: Our worldly associations and acquisitions are of no value to us when we face the call of Death. It is only the good that we do here that will help us in the journey beyond life into death.

In the *Upanishads*, a beautiful story is told to us about Rishi Yagnavalkya and his wife Maitreyi. Maitreyi was a remarkable woman – one in a million.

One day, the *rishi* said to his wife, "Dear one, my spiritual aspirations incline me to take up *sanyas*, the life of renunciation. I am concerned about your well-being, as I shall have to leave you behind. But here is a good amount of gold that will enable you to live in comfort. Grant me leave to take up the quest that my soul desires."

The wise woman that she was, Maitreyi said to her husband, "Swami, you are leaving behind a great deal of gold, which is very valuable. And you say you go in search of something else that your heart desires. Am I right in assuming then, that what you seek is far more valuable than gold? Would you please tell me what is this precious thing that you seek, which all this gold cannot buy?"

"My quest is for Liberation, to attain the Lotus Feet of the Lord, beyond the heaven world," replied Rishi Yagnavalkya. "It is a state that transcends grief and death. No amount of gold can buy this for me. Now that you know what I seek, will you let me go?"

"If that which you seek is more valuable than all this gold," said Maitreyi, "I do not wish to settle for this gold. Let us leave this gold behind, for I wish to join you in your spiritual quest."

Human life is a rare and precious gift that has been bestowed upon us by God, so that we may attain salvation and reach Him. Lord Jesus tells us that the man who runs after the world is enchained by the world; he who drinks the salty water of the sea to quench his thirst, will find that he will bloat with the salt water, unable to slake his thirst.

Thus it is that man drives himself towards disaster. If only he could open his eyes to the truth, he will realise that this world is but a bridge which he has to cross in order to reach his Beloved. In the beautiful words of the *Nuri Granth*, Gurudev Sadhu Vaswani tells us:

"O, dear one! The Ocean of divine comfort is before you. Do not go away thirsty from its shore."

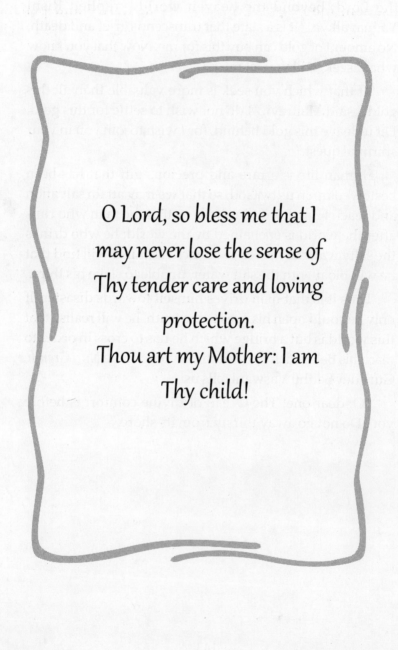

O Lord, so bless me that I may never lose the sense of Thy tender care and loving protection.
Thou art my Mother: I am Thy child!

The Gift God Needs

Today, my thoughts fly back to the year 1945, when Gurudev Sadhu Vaswani was invited to the Banaras Hindu University. Pandit Madan Mohan Malaviya was the Chancellor of the University at that time. He requested Gurudev Sadhu Vaswani to visit the University and address the professors and students on ancient Indian ideals and values.

Situated close to Banaras is the well-known historic location of Sarnath, one of the main pilgrimage centres associated with Gautama Buddha. It is here that the famous Mulagandhakuti Vihara, a distinguished Buddhist Monastery is located. This monastery is of considerable historic and religious significance. It was here that the Buddha first taught the *dhamma*, and it was here that the Buddhist *Sangha* came into existence. Allow me to narrate to you the wonderful story of how it all came to pass.

During those long, hard years when he was seeking enlightenment in the *tapobana* – the forest of meditation, Gautama had as his companions, five *tapasvis* who looked upon him as their leader and mentor. Gautama had at that time undertaken to perform severe austerities and penance, as he felt this was the right way to enlightenment. During the course of his severe *tapasya*, the song of a young maiden fell on his ears: "Tune the sitar neither low nor high." These words brought home to him the great truth that severe austerity and penance would not lead him to the enlightenment he sought. The strings of the sitar need to be stretched just right – neither too tight, nor too slack – if they are to produce melodious music. It seemed to Gautama that he had stretched himself beyond the limit with severe austerities. He now had to unwind the tightened strings – tune them right, neither too high, nor too low.

The realisation dawned on him that mortification of the body was not always equivalent to the elevation of the mind. How could enlightenment be attained by one who has lost his strength and is wearied with hunger, thirst and fatigue, while his mind was weakened by utter exhaustion of the body?

When this awareness came to him, Gautama accepted with gratitude the sweetened rice and milk offered to him by a lady called Sujata. This marked a new direction for his quest, and the end of his severe asceticism. But this was met with utter disapproval by his five companions, who left him in disgust, vowing never to meet him or talk to him ever again. As for Gautama, he took his seat in the lotus posture under the tree at Bodh Gaya, vowing that he would not get up until he had found the truth he was seeking. And so it came to pass that on the Full Moon Day of the month of Visaka (May) which we now celebrate as Buddha Purnima, Gautama attained enlightenment.

When he became the Buddha or the Enlightened One, he realised that people were entrapped in a vicious cycle of sorrow and suffering. The main reason for this was *trishna*, worldly desire. He felt therefore, that if only man could control his desire, it was possible for him to become liberated from human sorrow and suffering. He decided that he would share the fruits of his great realisation, the knowledge of his enlightenment, with the rest of humanity, so that this may enable people to seek liberation from sorrow.

With this noble intention, he set out to teach his ideals to seeking souls.

It was at Sarnath that he began his sacred mission. On reaching Sarnath, he met the five *tapasvis*, who had turned their backs on him when he gave up his extreme asceticism. Now, on seeing Gautama face to face at Sarnath, they said to each other, "Here comes Gautama. We will stand by our earlier decision to have nothing to do with him; we shan't even look at him." But as they drew closer to the Buddha, they were so dazzled by the radiance that seemed to emanate from his eyes. They forgot all their earlier animosity towards him, and decided to dedicate their lives to his service. One of them picked up his *kamandal*, another bowed in reverence before him, and all five sought to become his disciples. There it was at the historic location of Sarnath that the Buddha delivered his first ever sermon on the Four Noble Truths of the *Dhamma*:

(1) There is suffering in human life

(2) This suffering has a cause

(3) The cause is removable

(4) There are ways to remove the causes.

So, to remove the causes the Buddha prescribed an Eight-fold Path: Right speech, Right action, Right livelihood, Right effort, Right mindfulness, Right concentration, Right attitude and Right view.

Here on the site of the deer park at Sarnath, in the third century BC, Emperor Ashoka erected a column of over 15 metres in height, topped by four lions, to symbolise both Ashoka's imperial rule and the kingship of the Buddha. The four-lion capital was adopted as the emblem of the modern Indian republic. Later, a huge Buddhist *vihaara* was erected to commemorate this sacred location, where the voice of Buddhism was first heard.

As I said, Gurudev Sadhu Vaswani was invited to visit Sarnath when we were at Banaras. I felt blessed to accompany him on this trip. It was truly a privilege to be with him and we traveled to the monastery on a *tonga*.

One of our fellow passengers was a learned pundit. He began to talk to me as we moved towards Sarnath. In the course of his conversation, he said to me, "May I tell you, young man, our *shastras* speak of five different attitudes of the devotee towards the Lord. The first is *Shanta bhava*; in this aspect, the devotee dwells in peace and true inner joy; the second is the *Daasya bhava*, in which the devotee assumes the role of the Lord's servant. Thus it was that Sri Hanuman regarded himself, first and foremost as Lord Ram's servant. The third is the *Saakhya bhava*, in which the devotee assumes the attitude of the *sakha* or friend. Arjun looked upon Sri Krishna as his dear friend. The fourth is the attitude of *Vatsalya bhava*, affection. To Yashoda *Mata*, Shyam Sundar was a beloved child. The fifth is the attitude of *Madhurya bhava*; here, the devotee looks upon the Lord as his Beloved, his Divine lover. Such was Radha's great love for Sri Krishna. The devotee who adopts the attitude of love, regards the Lord as his all – as the light of his life, as life itself."

Having explained the five different attitudes to the Lord, the *pundit* asked me with a smile, "Now tell me, which of these attitudes has your Gurudev adopted? How does your beloved Master look upon the Lord?"

"That is for the Master himself to say," I replied in all humility. "But to my knowledge, Gurudev Sadhu Vaswani's approach to God is not one among the five you just mentioned."

"How could that be?" said the pundit, dismayed. "Is there a sixth *bhava* that I do not know of?"

"Undoubtedly there is," I assured him, in all the confidence of my youth. (For I was barely 30 years old at that time.) "If I must put a name to it, I think I should call it the *Maatru bhava* – for I do believe that our Gurudev looks upon the Lord as his Divine Mother. He tells all of us to regard the Lord as our own Mother, and to call out to Her in love, devotion and reverence, as a child calls out to its mother."

The pundit nodded his head in approval of what I had said. "True it is," he remarked thoughtfully, "we say in our prayers, *Tum mata pita, hum baalak tere…*"

When we look upon God as our Mother, we will have no hesitation whatsoever in approaching Her in all conditions and all circumstances of life. No other attitude will enable us to feel the same intimacy and proximity with the Lord as this, which is called *Maatru bhava*.

"*Twameva mata cha pita Twameva*" runs the famous prayer. God is our Beloved Mother; He is also our dear Father. If we look upon Him as our Mother, we will experience a distinct closeness to Him.

Human beings are constantly swept and tossed by the storm of desires. These desires drag us into the filth of sin and evil. We are stained by our own evil doings. Therefore people say, "God is all Purity, Light and Radiance. How can we approach Him, covered as we are in the stench and filth of sin?"

Just think of a little child who falls down in a puddle of muddy water, when he is playing. His clothes are mud-splattered; his face and hands and feet are filthy. But he runs to his mother without fear and tells her, "Maa, I've become so dirty! Wash my hands and feet. Clean me." For the little child, there is no hesitation, no embarrassment in turning to the mother. So it should be with us. If our lives are stained and become impure with the evil of sin, we should turn to God without fear or hesitation.

Indeed, our condition is akin to the filthy child. We are led astray by desires and by the pull of our own sensual pleasures, and fall into the terrible mire of sin. We too, should call out to God like the little child, "Maa, Maa! Cleanse me! Wash me in the Divine waters of Your Love and Mercy! Make me pure and clean! Give me the strength to resist evil and sin, so that I may always remain pure and stain-free!"

If only we approach God in this attitude of the child, we shall find wonders, miracles happening in our daily lives.

Sri Ramakrishna Paramahansa was a devotee of Goddess Kali. He attained God-realisation by looking upon the Lord as his Mother. Often, in deep ecstasy, he would call out, "*Maa, Maa!*" and thus calling out to the Divine Mother, he would enter the state of *samadhi* – deep bliss. Other great souls like the Shaivaite Naayanmaar saints of

South India have also adopted the same relationship with God as their loving Mother.

The Love between mother and child is indeed unique – it is the most loving, the most special relationship. If we call out to God as a child calls out to its mother, we cannot remain far from Her!

A little child was left to play with a few toys, while its mother was busy in the kitchen. The mother was making *kheer*, and had to keep constant watch over the boiling milk. All of a sudden, the child began to cry. The mother came running out of the kitchen, pacified the child and gave him a few more toys to play with. She then went back to the kitchen to attend to her tasks. But in a very short while, the child began to cry once again. This happened repeatedly. The child would cry; the mother would come running to pacify him; she would give him a few more toys and return to her work; the child would be quiet for a while, and then start crying for its mother.

A time comes when the child does not rest content with the toys given to him. He seems to cry out to his mother, "Maa, I do not want these toys. I want you! I need you! Only you can make me happy – not all the toys in the world!"

We are content to play with toys most of the time – our wealth, our possessions, our children, our parents, our spouses, our jobs, our factories, our business – for what are all these, but toys that our loving Mother, God has given to us in Her love and affection! We are so, happy playing with these "toys" that we forget God. But there are a few among us who do not rest content with these toys. Like the persistent child, they cry out to God, "Mother, we want You and You alone!"

No mother can bear to hear her child cry. She comes out rushing to lift the child and wipe away his tears and pacify him with her tender touch. She carries the child in her arms and holds the child close to her heart.

A young girl was on a holiday, travelling across the European continent. When she was in Italy, she remembered that her mother's birthday was drawing near. She went shopping for a special gift, and purchased a very expensive cut-glass table lamp. She wrapped it up carefully and exquisitely. She sent the parcel to her mother.

The parcel reached the mother on her birthday. The mother opened the parcel and saw the exquisite crystal lamp. Her eyes were touched with tears, as she penned a note to her daughter: "My dear child, I thank you for the beautiful gift you have sent me. But the truth is that I do not need such expensive gifts. I want you – only you!"

God is our Loving Mother. He tells us: "My dear Children, you visit temples, you undertake pilgrimages, you perform *pujas* and *yagnas*. These are all gifts that you offer at My feet. But I do not want these offerings. All I want is you -- and only you!"

A mother's heart always calls out to her children; she longs to be with her child. So too, God, our Loving Mother, calls out to us: "All I need is your loving heart."

Alas, our hearts are enamoured of worldly matters and worldly pleasures. When we learn to rise above these worldly desires, we surrender our hearts at the Lord's feet. Then the currents of our consciousness will constantly flow in the direction of God. Let us surrender our hearts at the Mother's feet! Let us offer our Divine Mother the best gift any mother can ever get – the gift of a loving heart!